SKETCHES FROM A LIFE

Also by Anne Scott-James

IN THE MINK

DOWN TO EARTH

SISSINGHURST – THE MAKING OF A GARDEN

THE PLEASURE GARDEN
(with Osbert Lancaster)

THE COTTAGE GARDEN

GLYNDEBOURNE: THE GARDENS
(with Christopher Lloyd)

THE LANGUAGE OF THE GARDEN

THE BEST PLANTS FOR YOUR GARDEN

THE BRITISH MUSEUM BOOK OF FLOWERS
(with Ray Desmond and Frances Wood)

GARDENING LETTERS TO MY DAUGHTER
(with Clare Hastings)

SKETCHES FROM A LIFE

Anne Scott-James

MICHAEL JOSEPH
London

Michael Joseph Ltd

Published by the Penguin Group
27 Wrights Lane, London W8 5TZ
Viking Penguin Inc., 375 Hudson Street, New York, New York 10014, USA
Penguin Books Australia Ltd, Ringwood, Victoria, Australia
Penguin Books Canada Ltd, 10 Alcorn Avenue, Toronto, Ontario, Canada M4V 3B2
Penguin Books (NZ) Ltd, 182–190 Wairau Road, Auckland 10, New Zealand

Penguin Books Ltd, Registered Offices: Harmondsworth, Middlesex, England

First published in Great Britain 1993

Printed and bound in Great Britain by
Butler & Tanner Ltd, Frome and London

A CIP catalogue record for this book is available from the British Library

ISBN 0 7181 3531 8

For my family

Acknowledgements

I would like to thank Jenny Dereham, editorial director of Michael Joseph, for supporting me with a rare combination of moral encouragement and practical help. My New York friends, Hank and Fanny Brennan, have jogged my memory about visits to the USA. My recollections of Nancy Mitford and of Moscow are based on an article I wrote for the *Sunday Express*, and of Kenya on a series published in the *Daily Mail*. Otherwise, I have relied on my own memory, and hope it has not proved too fallible.

Contents

List of Illustrations

All the line drawings are by Osbert Lancaster. Those on pages 177 and 179 appeared in his book *Sailing to Byzantium*, published by John Murray.

Dear Clare,

I am determined never to be a boring old lady pinning reluctant listeners to stories of my youth, like the ancient mariner and the wedding guest. But to my surprise, you love looking through my family photographs and often quiz me about my childhood, which seems only yesterday to me, but has a period charm for you. You ask me, too, about my life when childhood was over and I became one of the first generation of career girls. As one yourself you can scarcely believe that in the 1930s a professional woman was something of an oddity. Was it an adventure or a struggle?

As you responded with such zest to my gardening letters that we made a book of them,* I thought I would begin writing again, each letter a flashback to my earlier life. I don't want them to be essays in egotism; they will be more like snapshots of the varied times I have lived through.

I have only dim infant memories of the First World War, but vivid recollections of the roaring twenties (which never roared for me), of Oxford in the thirties (then a gloomy, conventual place for women), of the happy release into the freedom of a job and a flat, then the rich experience of *Picture Post* in the last war, and marriage, children and an exhilarating career thereafter, with world-wide travelling and acres of newspaper space to fill with my exuberant opinions.

Although my base has always been London, many of my clearest mental flashbacks are of the country. I could map the woods where I picked wild flowers as a child and I could make an index of all the plans and plants which have gone to make the garden of Rose Cottage, my country refuge for more than fifty years. Most lives are untidy, and mine is no exception, a mixture of happiness and misery, success and failure, false starts and strokes of luck, but it has rarely been boring. I hope my letters will interest you because they touch on quite a wide range of experience, and because they will be as true as I can make them, without self-praise or 'touching up'.

Your loving Mother.

**Gardening Letters to my Daughter*, Michael Joseph, 1990.

Out of the Mists

My memories of the First World War are nebulous, as I was only one year old in 1914, so I will hurry past them. I remember that my father, a captain in the Royal Artillery, was mostly at the front, where he won the MC, and I lived in our small terraced house in Bayswater with my mother, my sister Marie, seven years older than I, my brother John, two years younger, and a nanny, and we spent occasional holidays in Berkshire. (We later learned that John was incurably epileptic, a shadow over all our lives, but we did not know it at this time.)

I don't know if there is a psychological explanation for this, but my clearest wartime memories are of being woken in the night. We children were woken if there was an air raid, wrapped in blankets and carried round to my grandparents, who lived in the next street in a flat with a basement, a reasonable protection against the sort of bombs which were dropped in the first war. We greatly enjoyed the excitement. I also remember being woken if my father arrived on leave, which was usually without warning. On one occasion we were all in the country, staying in a cottage which was to be the scene of many later holidays, and my father had a terrible job to find us, having arrived late at night at Reading station, seven miles away. He could get no transport and had to tramp along the country roads to our hamlet, which was unknown to him. We were all indignant when he told us that he had knocked up the landlady of a country pub called the Rising Sun two miles from our lodgings, who was so cross at being woken that she refused to give him directions. At last he reached us and received welcoming hugs. Many country people in that war, being perfectly safe, wrapped themselves in a cocoon of selfishness, but in the last war most experiences were widely shared and people were more generous to each other.

The only other thing I remember about my life up to the age of five was getting into a temper and cutting a hated pair of knickers to pieces. They were green stockinette and laddered delightfully as I snipped, but the retributions were frightful. We were not a smacking family; our punishments were cancelled treats, and I was deprived of a longed-for children's Christmas party. I could not even accidentally break a cup or glass with impunity, and even today the smashing of crockery, which gets such a laugh in a TV sit-com, gets only a shudder from me. I was frightened of my parents, being born too soon for Dr Spock. I caught the tail end of the Victorian philosophy that parents were perfect, and children always in the wrong, a righteous target for round-the-clock criticism. This made me very shy in company, and as a child I had none of the social ease of my lucky grandchildren, who assume unless it is proved to the contrary that grown-ups are their friends.

A Crazy Village

In 1920 I reached the age of seven, and the pictures of my childhood come into sharper focus, though they are without continuity, making more of a magic lantern show than a film.

I remember the country more vividly than London because I adored the Berkshire village where I spent many school holidays, always with John, who was in my care once we were past the nanny years, and occasionally with Marie, too, though the gap in our ages was too large for us to form a team. The village was Burghfield Common, seven miles south-west of Reading, poised on a gravel plateau above the Kennet valley, into which many little streams poured their clear water. This was pine-tree country, with acres of gorse and heather and village ponds enlivened with water plants – crowfoot and arrowhead and the carnivorous sundew which fascinated me, because it ate insects. The whole of Burghfield is now built over, a dormitory town for Reading.

Sometimes we stayed in the village inn, the Three Firs, kept by Mr and Mrs Gibbons, who managed the inn and its small surrounding farm where I mixed pigwash in a tub, fed the chickens and collected the eggs, which were laid all over the place, even in the hedges. The inn revelled in the luxury of indoor plumbing, and a boiler was lit once a week to heat our Saturday bath water. Sometimes we stayed in the nearby village of Sulhamstead, where the vegetation was much lusher. The woods were oak, not pine, full of violets and primroses, solomon's seal and orchids, and runnelled with streams. There was a marshy place with pale marsh violets and wild balsam.

Here we lodged in a semi-detached cottage in the care of the fierce, moustachioed old lady who owned it, Mrs Cooper, former nanny to a lordly family in Ireland, so she was more than able to keep us in order. My parents did not accompany us on our Berkshire holidays, which were usually in the spring, but reserved their strength for a family seaside holiday in August.

Mrs Cooper was a fine old-fashioned country cook who made perfect pastry, grew vegetables and kept chickens, which she herself slaughtered with relish when required for the pot, but the cottage was poky, the small parlour crammed with Victorian pictures, china, texts and calendars which we derided, though they would fetch a fortune today. I particularly disliked a large engraving of a small boy in a velvet Lord Fauntleroy outfit, entitled *His First Suit*. The plumbing consisted of a hip-bath which we took once a week in the kitchen, one after another in the same hot water, and an outside privy, with a pile of squares cut out of the *Daily Mail* for loo paper. A bucket of ashes stood by the lavatory and after using it we put a scoopful of ashes down the pan as a germ-killer. None of this seemed any hardship, a small price to pay for the joys of the country. We had no car, of course, but walked everywhere, and it is only by walking that one gets to know a district and its inhabitants intimately. I knew every cottage, every bird's nest, every wild flower within our little territory. Sometimes I would leave John at the cottage and go further afield on a borrowed bicycle, with a collecting tin slung round my neck for flowers. I would press them in the evenings in blotting paper, and sort and label them when dry.

For me, the country was never a slow cabbagey sort of place, but was rich in incident, and though I didn't understand it at the time, I realize now that many of the country people we knew were absolutely cracked.

Mrs Higgins, up the road, who took in washing, committed suicide by swallowing a bottle of Condy's Fluid, a strong disinfectant. Of course I was not told this, but I was an eager listener to the gossip of Mrs Cooper and her cronies, and it did not take long to put two and two together. ('Sharp' they called me.) The recourse to Condy's Fluid was regarded as a wicked act, especially as Mrs Higgins had a young family ('She should have thought of the poor little mites'), and I have no idea what drove her to it. I did, however, know why poor Mr Gibbons of the Three Firs shot himself. It was money. The farm was failing. His wife was a bitter old woman who had no children, but had a niece to live in the inn, who was treated like a slave. She never had a day off, was never allowed to go into the town, just scrubbed and washed and cleaned every hour of every day, and churned the butter once a week, a stiff task with a hand-churn. She was given neither wage nor pocket money, and when my father once came to collect us and gave her a secret tip, it was discovered and taken away. Nellie was in her late twenties, and could have taken herself off, but had been cowed into subjection. So that family was pretty cracked, too.

So was the vicar of nearby Ufton church, a highly educated man of a distinguished clerical family, but burdened with too many children and a defeated wife. He went about in threadbare clothes with holes in his socks, cackling and muttering to himself. The children had barely enough to eat, but when the parson had parishioners to tea a generous meal was laid on – my sister Marie, seven years older and wiser than I, told me to restrain my greed and confine myself to one chocolate biscuit and one piece of cake. Sometimes we invited the children, seven in all, I think, to tea at our cottage and Mrs Cooper provided a splendid meal, which the children fell upon like wolves. The vicar had a passion for tennis, and there was a bumpy, weedy grass court in the vicarage garden, and as he had no tennis shoes he played in his socks, and the holes were embarrassingly obvious. Have you ever in your life mended socks or tights? Today, when they develop ladders or potatoes, they go in the dustbin, but in those days darning socks and stockings was a never-ending occupation.

I don't say that the gamekeeper of the local estate was cracked, but it was rumoured that his wife beat him, although he was a robust man who looked tough enough, with his gun and gaiters, to resist. We liked him because he allowed us to spend long hours in the woods on our own except when the pheasants were nesting. Apart from these positively eccentric characters there were, of course, two or three children in the village who were simple.

All this, you might think, was in the middle of the nineteenth century, but no, I am writing of the 1920s. It was not until the advent of the popular motor-car (we bought our first Morris in 1935) that the countryside entered modern times, and country people were less lonely. There were still maniacs in plenty in Stella Gibbons' immortal *Cold Comfort Farm*, published in 1932.

First School

I feel quite embarrassed in telling you that I loved my schooldays. Nearly every literate Englishman seems to have been bullied, beaten and humiliated at school, to have loathed playing games, to have been taught nothing but rubbish, forcibly fed with useless facts,and to have been at the mercy of sadistic schoolmasters and beefy prefects. Turning the pages of their memoirs has made my heart bleed in turn for Orwell, Betjeman, Waugh, John Mortimer, the two Osberts – O. Sitwell and my future husband, O. Lancaster – and a hundred other sensitive boys locked in a barbarous environment. Of course, the poor little blighters were sent to boarding schools and I went to two London day schools. (I was not shut up until I went to Oxford, which I disliked intensely, so I do understand the frustrations of imprisonment.) But why were they *all* so bad at games? Surely there must be an occasional intellectual who enjoyed playing cricket or even rowing or football? I think it was team games which disgusted these individualists, for Betjeman later became a dab at golf and Lancaster claimed he could ski, though there are no living witnesses.

My first school, which I attended from four-and-a-half to ten years old, was Norland Place School in Holland Park, and very good it was. It was a girls-only school, except in the bottom form where there were a few boys, for in private schools co-education was still rare, and regarded as 'advanced', not to say cranky.

I started in the kindergarten and enjoyed it from the first day, when a new creative world of making things with my hands opened to me. We made splashy pictures with poster paints and learned clay modelling and basket-weaving – our poor mothers were all given Christmas presents of cane 'hair-tidies' which were squalid receptacles for hair combings intended to ornament the dressing-table. But we also learned spelling and counting and we could all read by five, or six at the latest, learning by the traditional method of making letters into syllables and syllables into words, then sentences – no baloney about flashcards or phonetics or just hoping that a child would want to read in his own good time, which might be never.

As we went up the school lessons were of course more varied. A curious assortment of educational scraps taught me at this period still sticks irrationally in my mind. Why do I remember after seventy years that the Portuguese, unlike the English, made bad colonists because they grew slack in hot climates and intermarried with the natives? Or that there are gentleman plants and lady plants and if the two get together they produce little plants? How they achieved this was not explained, and we children had no inkling of the facts of sex or reproduction, and I don't suppose our botany mistress knew much more.

But it is unfair to laugh at these trivia. It is not surprising if the English were a little jingoistic so soon after winning the war, and the discretion of the botany mistress was typical of its time – there would have been outraged complaints from parents if we had been given even the most elementary sex instruction. In general, the teaching at Norland Place was first-class, as it is today. We had a specialized mistress for most subjects, including a genuine mam'selle for French, and never suffered the monotony of one all-purpose teacher taking every subject.

When I first went to school I tagged along with my elder sister Marie, but after she left and went on to St Paul's, I went alone. I used to pocket the money given me for my bus fares and spend it on sweets and walked home with a gang of friends, so that I was always late for tea and my mother was always cross with me. It is hard to believe today that quite young children could travel about London alone in the 1920s. There were no school buses, no mothers sharing the school run by car, nor conscientious fathers dropping their offspring at school on their way to the City, for these precautions were not needed.

Through all my time at Norland Place, I had been the youngest in my class by a year or more, and when, at ten, I passed into St Paul's, the same thing happened and I was put into a form with twelve-year-olds. There seemed to be a general agreement that 'Anne needs to be extended', like a victim of Procrustes' bed. I am afraid that I owed my precocity more to a phenomenal short-term memory (quite gone today) than to virtuous application or profundity of thought.

One minor annoyance of spending my life with older girls caused me some pain. My parents insisted on dressing me to my age, not my position in the school, and decreed a bedtime much earlier than that of my friends. Even at Norland Place my best friend told me that my clothes were babyish, and I still wore boots – good for the ankles – when all the others wore strap shoes. At St Paul's, I had the misery of going to parties in a short-sleeved dress with a gathered waist when my friends wore sleeveless flapper dresses with no waist at all and an artificial gardenia on the shoulder. But these were bearable irritants in a school life which I remember with pleasure.

Great-aunt Eleanor

My father, whom you scarcely knew, was the son of a poor parson, a minister in the Congregational church who contrived, through a strict economy of living, to educate his large family of two sons and six daughters, mostly on scholarships – my father was a classical scholar of Brasenose College, Oxford. The family was high-minded and conscientious, my father later making a distinguished name as a literary critic and my aunts, nearly all of them spinsters, making careers in far-flung quarters of the world as teachers, or, in one case, as a nun. Serious people.

My mother's family was more sophisticated, with wealth and a county background on both paternal and maternal sides, though hunting, gambling and general extravagance had dissipated most of the money before Mother's marriage to Daddy. My mother had charm and wit, and though never formally educated, was a natural writer who took to writing newspaper articles after her marriage to add to the family income and eventually wrote an excellent regular 'London Letter' for the *Yorkshire Post*. The most respected figure in my mother's family was her mother's sister, my great-aunt Eleanor, whose code of propriety left an indelible mark on my mother, on me, and even on you, Clare, who were born more than twenty years after she died in her nineties.

Aunt Eleanor must have been born in the 1840s, and remained every inch a Victorian. She married a well-to-do old Etonian, Laurence Craven, a man of taste and scholarship who I think died young, for when I first knew my great-aunt she had long been a widow, unfortunately childless, a tiny, but stately little woman whose manners, habits and fashions never changed an iota after her husband's death. She wore long black or grey dresses over petticoats, high wired Edwardian collars, a diamond brooch, doeskin gloves and highly polished buckled shoes over black open-work stockings, and her hair was piled into an elaborate coiffure which I later learned was a toupée. She was a religious woman, strictly Church of England, the only unkind feeling in her heart being a fanatical hatred of Roman Catholics. I only recently worked out a possible reason for this intolerance. Her ancestors had been Huguenots called de Métevier, who fled from France after the repeal of the Edict of Nantes in 1685, so perhaps she associated Catholics with persecution. But again, there was a strong no-Popery tide of feeling in England in her youth which may have swept her away.

From a date long before I was born, Aunt Eleanor lived in a vast Edwardian flat in Westminster among fine carpets and chandeliers, furniture of museum quality, exquisite porcelain, *objets d'art* and silver, and surprisingly good pictures which her husband must have collected, for my aunt cared only for the Royal Academy and never missed a summer opening. Marie and I used to take luncheon with her every other Sunday when we were in London, and the occasion was in many ways a treat, for the food was delicious, always loin of lamb from the Army and Navy Stores, home-made jellies, ice-cream and lemonade. We liked being waited on by the starched parlour-maid, and we were usually given a box of Mackintosh's toffee to take home. But the atmosphere was dauntingly formal. We were reproved for using slang words, like 'tophole' and 'ripping' and 'she's a beast', for being untidy and for any fault in manners. We spent the hours between lunch and tea resting, the only amusements being a solitaire board and the latest number of the *Sphere*. I once took my favourite journal with me for afternoon reading, *Tiger Tim's Weekly*, with its entrancing comic adventures of Tiger Tim and the Bruin Boys, but this was put away and returned to me in silence when we left. There was much kindness in the air, but not much laughter.

On one occasion, probably my birthday, Aunt Eleanor took me to the theatre, and I had chosen, prompted doubtless by my parents, to see a play by Christopher Morley called *Thunder on the Left*. Owing to some verbal misunderstanding with the ticket agency, my aunt had taken a box for Ben Travers' rollicking farce *Plunder*, then playing at the Aldwych, with the accomplished team of Ralph Lynn, Robertson Hare, Mary Brough and Winifred Shotter running in and out of bedrooms in various states of undress. I was enjoying myself enormously until the delectable Winifred Shotter's skirt came off in the hands of Robertson Hare, leaving her standing in pink silk knickers, when Aunt Eleanor took me firmly by the arm and marched me out of the theatre.

It was from Aunt Eleanor that I learned about etiquette – next to religion, the most important thing in life was to behave like a lady. 'A lady never makes personal remarks.' 'A lady never mentions the food at luncheon.' 'A lady always wears gloves.' 'A lady never uses printed writing-paper, it must be die-stamped.' When Nancy Mitford's U and non-U came out, I knew it all already. You, dear child, may protest that no residue from Aunt Eleanor's code remains in our family, but you are wrong. True, you never wear gloves except woolly ones for warmth, you talk about food at meals, and speak slang as a second language. But you never get drunk, you never say 'pleased to meet you', your silver is polished, your bedspreads are real linen, and as soon as she could lisp Calypso* was meticulous in saying 'please' and 'thank you'.

I do not know how Aunt Eleanor would have coped with modern travel. Every winter she took rooms in Bath or Ventnor in the Isle of Wight and went for three months, taking a maid and a high proportion of her worldly goods. She travelled with ten pieces of luggage of the heaviest leather, ranging from large trunks down to a dressing-case, plus her parrot in a cage. A porter was secured on her arrival at the London railway station and stayed with her until she was safely in her first-class carriage, the luggage being stowed in the van and the guard instructed to keep a personal watch on it. Occasionally Marie and I were invited to join her for a week, but I must admit that we were intensely bored. Like most children, we were financially grasping, and the best thing about these visits was that my aunt would give each of us a substantial tip.

Aunt Eleanor was extremely generous with her money to her large circle of nephews and nieces and their offspring. Though her own formal education was scanty, she believed in a better one for the younger generation, including the girls, and no great-nephew or great-niece was kept from the university for lack of funds. She also contributed to family crises, such as an operation or the death of a breadwinner.

When Aunt Eleanor's memory slipped away in old age, my mother was deputed by all the cousins to look after her household. My mother was too neurotic to be good with

*Clare's daughter, born in 1980.

children and I would say that we three were definitely neglected, but she was surprisingly patient with old people in their second childhood. She visited Aunt Eleanor regularly, engaged her staff, and arranged for her flat and wardrobe to be elegant to the last. The only difference I remember in my aunt's latter-day appearance was that her toupée was replaced by her natural hair, which was wavy and silvery and just as attractive.

Mr Taylor and His Women

Mr Taylor was my first conscious contact with 'the poor' who, in the 1920s, made up a large part of the population of London. But 'the poor' were not visible unless you looked for them, for they lived in unofficial ghettos, emerging rarely except to go to work. They shopped in their own street markets, there being no democratic Tesco or Safeway at that period where all sorts meet. Our nearest poor neighbours inhabited the slummy streets of Notting Dale, which were like the back streets of Naples without the sunshine. In one of these lived the Taylor family.

Mr Taylor – I never learned his Christian name – was our 'little man', or odd-job-man, and it was often my task to fetch him from his home when our lights failed, the sink was stopped up, or a sashcord broke in one of the windows. Mr Taylor did a little bit of everything, observing no demarcation rules, but he did nothing well, and it was not uncommon for his repairs to fall apart before the door closed behind him. However, we continued to use him because he was unemployed, always available, and reasonably honest.

Mr Taylor was a little man in more senses than one. He was physically small and weedy, probably not much more than five feet tall, with a few blackened teeth. He wore the same greasy suit and waistcoat through all the years of our acquaintance, smoked Woodbines, whined a bit, sniffed a bit, and seemed to the casual eye singularly unattractive though, as I will relate, he turned out to be something of a Don Juan. The happiest years of his life had been in the First World War, when he had been a private in France, sharing the comradeship of men, fed and clothed by the army, and free of all responsibilities. I did not enjoy going to fetch him, for it involved a dreary walk to the depressing basement where he lived in crowded squalor with his wife, Emily, her unmarried sister, Rose, and eight children, and I would have to chat to the family for a few minutes for politeness' sake. Most of the children were dressed in our outworn clothes and there would be bits of familiar crockery on the table.

Mrs Taylor was the most attractive member of the family. She was Welsh and, though dirty and weary-looking, was remarkably beautiful, with the high cheekbones and consumptive pallor which I was to see in later life in the Welsh mining valleys. She had a mass of tangled dark hair. She was an extraordinarily good cook, better than any regular cook in our employment, and would sometimes come to help with our rare dinner parties, or take over if the usual cook was on holiday. Unfortunately, her visits were also in the nature of raids, her loot being sheets from the linen cupboards, clothes, or tins of food, and we simply could not afford the losses. Once my mother was bold enough to challenge her. I had seen Emily in her home wearing my mother's best jersey, for which she had been looking in vain for days, and as we were all fed up with turning out cupboards and drawers and going through the linen basket, I thought I had better report it. Questioned politely by my mother, who said that if Emily had taken it she was sure it was a misunderstanding, Emily coolly replied that we owned so much more than she did that she felt it right to take her share. My mother was floored. She often said she would never have Emily in the house again, but when she wanted some divine pastry, or a melting rabbit stew for the weekend, I would be sent round with a message. 'Ladies' did not cook in those days; my mother never learned to scramble an egg, and I did not cook until the war taught us all to make allegedly delicious dishes out of such novelties as whalemeat or Spam.

After knowing the Taylors for several years, thinking of them with pity but not, I am afraid, with affection, I went round one afternoon on my usual errand to find a raging row going on in their one living-room. Emily was throwing saucepans at her sister, Rose, and the children were screaming. Mr Taylor was out. I retreated home. The mystery was soon unravelled, and though we children were not supposed to know it, the story filtered through.

It appeared that Mr Taylor had, not for weeks, but for years, been having an affair with Rose, who had none of her sister's good looks, but was not worn out with child-bearing and feeding eight children on a pound or two a week, so perhaps had more energy for sex. On the day of my ill-starred visit, Emily had cracked, made a gigantic scene, and insisted on Rose leaving the house. The final revelation was that Mr Taylor and

Emily were not married, anyway, so I suppose Mr Taylor could have gone off with Rose had he wished, but he was much too frightened of Emily, or perhaps (our imaginations soared) had a legal wife in the background whom he had abandoned. Rose did in fact retire from the scene for several months, though she came back later. My father, who rarely laughed, was so overcome by the irony of this strange triangle, so unsuspected by us, that he 'gave way to mirth', as I. Compton-Burnett would have put it. My own sympathies were with Emily, who made our birthday-cakes and was high-spirited, and altogether more likeable than her sister.

If I sound heartless about the Taylors, it is not because of their squalor. A few years later I came to know many East End families through St Paul's school, which helped to finance a settlement in Stepney in which I took a deep interest, visiting it whenever I could and making real friends, rejecting my mother's protests that I might 'catch something'. I think the Taylors were just too hardened to help, too self-absorbed to love, and they had no cockney humour to lighten their burdens and our guilt. Or perhaps the chore of fetching the odd-job man was just so dreary that it put me off the whole family.

St Paul's

From the ages of ten to eighteen I went to St Paul's Girls' School, and I am going to put myself for ever among the philistines by saying how much I enjoyed it, especially the games. Tennis, netball and gym were the high spots of my day. I was proud of my St Trinian's uniform of gym tunic and black stockings which gave me the feeling, so necessary to a child, of belonging to a community. Later, in adolescence, when one struggles for personal identity, we were allowed to wear what we liked, and we seniors preened ourselves in shiny pink stockings and clinging stockinette jumper suits which revealed our figures – some too bumpy, some, like mine, not bumpy enough – all too clearly. In this matter of uniform, as in so much else, St Paul's was an enlightened and liberal establishment, years ahead of its time.

Academically, our reputation was awesome, but today our teaching would seem much too specialized. I left knowing no science at all. Most of us came from literary or political families, imbued with the traditions of history, English and the classics, and we felt no deprivation at the time. After taking matriculation (roughly the equivalent of O-level) in six or seven subjects, we specialized in the ones we had chosen for the university, keeping on a few extra arts subjects, such as French or German, but dropping maths and science, so that in maths I never got beyond logarithms and mastered not a molecule of physics or chemistry. Today I am a lost soul in the world of science, and especially of computers, and find this isolating – it is nothing to be proud of. To be mystified, as I am, by the slightly sinister magic of the fax machine and the credit card, to stare from the outside at a whole new world which one will never enter, gives one a faint idea of what it must be like to be illiterate.

St Paul's was known as a brainy school and we collected our full share of scholarships, but I don't remember the exam pressures which cause such stress today. The terrors of parent power were unknown and parents were never seen at school except on Speech Day. Most of us passed our exams, some failed and either took them again or changed course and turned to music, acting (I had a crush on a tall, leggy senior with enormous eyes called Celia Johnson) or athletics. They suffered no stigma or sense of doom. Of my best friends one was an academic genius, one became a Wimbledon tennis player. The musical standard of the school was outstanding, and our Master of Music was Gustav Holst, who conducted the school choir, sometimes played the organ at prayers, with panache rather than accuracy, and occasionally treated us to a solo on the trombone. We all adored him.

But within the academic set, we were frightful snobs. We thought the only worthwhile subjects were classics, mathematics, history and possibly English. We had the utmost contempt for science (which was indeed badly taught), and the dim, spotty few who studied chemistry or geography were, I fear, treated with politeness rather than warmth. We never dreamed that they would eclipse us thirty years on. My own subject was classics, and though our classics mistress, Miss Rogers, a plump, stately spinster known inevitably as Podge, was not, I think, very strong academically, she was a born teacher with a passion for Greek and Latin which she passed on to us. Nothing that she taught seemed dry; we laughed over the *Birds* (bowdlerized) and wept over the *Antigone*. She wore bright embroidered cardigans over her long swishing dresses and many rows of amber necklaces with which she fiddled so that they were always breaking, and many lessons were interrupted while we crawled round the floor picking up the beads.

Her whole class of six specialists got into Oxford or Cambridge, with two scholarships (one, oh happiness and bliss, was mine) and one exhibition, and as a goodbye present we took her out to dinner and the theatre. Predictably she chose Dodie Smith's *Autumn Crocus*, a sentimental play about a schoolmistress, played by Fay Compton, who fell in hopeless love with an innkeeper in the Austrian Tyrol. We gave her dinner in Soho first at Beguinot's, a French restaurant where you got a good four-course meal for half-a-crown, and we tactfully pretended not to notice when she took out her handkerchief in the course of the play.

One thing I still regret is that, although we were a young offshoot of St Paul's Boys' School, and were sponsored by the same City company, the Mercers, we had no communication with the boys, and shared none of their activities – the sexes were educated in Muslim isolation. The boys' school (now moved) was then cheek by jowl with ours, but the boys gawped at us as though we were animals in a zoo. The result was that, except for the lucky girls with older brothers, we grew up in half-frightened ignorance of boys and men.

In our last year at school, most of us felt that seventeen was too old for living in a one-sex society, and we wanted to move on. We complained bitterly to each other about the shortage of young men as dancing partners and had callow longings for a romantic friendship, Hollywood-style, with some charming hero who would kiss one lightly on the cheek, send one bouquets of flowers, and take one on a platonic trip to Paris. So total was our innocence that I thought of marriage as a specially pleasant form of social life, which would seem strange to the present generation of school-children who are accustomed to having condoms handed round with the exercise books. As for homosexuality, I had never heard of it.

It was only in my last year, when I was seventeen, that boredom crept into my enjoyment of my school days. Looking back, as we all do, on a chequered life, I remember St Paul's as one of the white squares.

A Modest Lifestyle

There must have been thousands of professional families who lived just like us in the 1920s, comfortable enough on moderate incomes, but with little in the way of luxury. Among respectable people it was a cardinal sin to get into debt, and this we never, ever did, spending only what we could afford, and solvency is built into my creed.

I'll tell you what our household was like in 1925, when I was twelve, John was ten, and Marie was in her second year at Oxford. We enjoyed the best in education, good family food and adequate domestic service, but against this there was a single iron-age bathroom, a flagstone floor in the kitchen, and no car, and we practised many household economies which would be pointless in today's throwaway society.

The house itself was charming, an early nineteenth-century terraced house in Bayswater. There was a small front garden planted with lilacs and bedding plants and a back garden with a lawn and an ash tree at the end. Mother and I managed the front garden, planting it with plants from a barrow which toured the streets on Saturdays – wallflowers, pansies, snapdragons, Canterbury bells; a man came in to mow the back lawn and Daddy watered it late at night, filling cans from the kitchen sink. It never occurred to us to install a hose.

The house was on three floors, with a drawing-room and dining-room downstairs divided by folding doors which, when opened, allowed a pleasant view from the front garden through to the greenery at the back. The drawing-room was decorated in the newly fashionable black and orange, with long linen curtains patterned with orange parrots and tropical flowers on a black ground. There was a central overhead light with a fringed black and orange shade. The dining-room had oak furniture and there was always a black Japanese open bowl in the centre of the table which held one kind of flower, Iceland poppies in season, then irises or chrysanthemums.

On the first floor was my parents' bedroom, my father's study, and the only bathroom, and above that were four small bedrooms, one for John, one shared by Marie and myself, with beds which folded against the wall by day, and one for the servant. I don't think she was allowed to use our bathroom, so I suppose she had a good wash from time to time at the washstand. The servant's lavatory was two floors down, off the kitchen. A living-in maid today, requiring 'own flat and TV' would scorn such primitive conditions, but we could always find a reasonably efficient cook-general, who was assisted by a daily char. Our house was so unmodernized, with no vacuum cleaner, central heating or planned kitchen, that it was absurdly labour-intensive, and help was essential. It was not until the last war that the middle classes learned that it was possible, even preferable, to live without service.

Some of our economies were quite daft. To avoid running up electricity bills, we paid by a shilling-in-the-slot meter and we were all instructed to collect shillings, but when the supply ran out and we were plunged into darkness, as often happened, none of us seemed to have the right coins. My father was supposed to top up the meter before one of our rare dinner parties, but once he forgot, and as the soup came in the lights went out. I was not present, being too young to stay up, but my mother said it was awkward, as the guests were visiting Americans, editors of the *Christian Science Monitor*, for which my father was writing some articles, and the blackout gave a bad impression. Electricity was held to be very expensive, and our bath water was heated by a noisy gas geyser, and electric lights were religiously switched off when not wanted. We children had no bedside lamps, so that if we read in bed one of us had to get out in the cold and switch off the light by the door, until I devised the ingenious system of jerking the switch off from my bed with a long string. One evening the jerk tore the switch off the wall with dreadful consequences. I had a strong Just William streak in those days.

Another economy was taxis – we took them only in case of illness or with luggage. We never ate in restaurants. On the other hand, we often went to the theatre, queueing for seats in the pit, which was very cheap. (The pit is now called back-of-the-stalls, and is very dear.) We went home afterwards by bus, for buses ran late.

We wore many secondhand clothes, but were not to be pitied, for one of my godmothers was a beautifully dressed woman with a constantly renewed wardrobe, who sent us parcels of clothes which were scarcely worn and often models. Mother, Marie and I divided the spoils, though I was often denied the dresses I wanted for they were 'too grown-up'. Once I was allowed a green taffeta backless dress which I coveted if I promised to fill in the back with green net. I did this, but made the inset removable, my naked back causing a sensation at the school dance. I was a good dressmaker, and we all spent hours mending stockings and altering clothes.

Our food was plentiful but plain, and we ate more than people eat today. We had four meals a day: a cooked breakfast, lunch, a serious tea with bread-and-butter and biscuits or cake, and supper, though this was light on weekdays, when my father was out at work leader-writing for his newspaper, the *Daily Chronicle*. The cooking was straightforward English family style, with a leg of Canterbury lamb every Sunday, beef not so often, chicken rarely for a treat. I also remember rabbit, Irish stew, fish pie, shepherd's pie and guinea-fowl, the poor man's pheasant. Puddings were such family standbys as jam sponge, baked apples, stewed fruit with custard, and pancakes. At tea, we children had to eat our first piece of bread and butter without jam, which was allowed with the second slice.

Tea, so rarely eaten now, at least in the south of England, was quite a social meal, and my mother had friends to tea more often than to dinner. On the other hand, friends in 'for drinks' was unknown. Alcohol was for dinner parties only, when there was sherry first, then some wine. My father always had a nightcap of whisky, otherwise tap water was the family drink, which I still think is a pleasant drink, if you can get it unpolluted. We were a non-alcoholic family from preference, not principle.

To my eye you, Clare, and your friends live extravagantly compared with us. You are not haunted, as we were, by dread of a rainy day. You have more comfortable homes, more cars, more clothes, more travel, a more sophisticated and a much more social way of life. On the other hand, you have to be able to turn your hand to anything from laundering to wood-chopping. At my age, the new do-it-yourself way is quite hard to learn, and faced with a dripping tap, a fused lamp or a Rawl-plug, I sometimes hanker for my childhood *bête-noire*, Mr Taylor, to help me with the odd jobs.

White Roads

I don't believe you have ever seen a true country road, I mean a rough white ribbon of stones and dust, like the roads in a Helen Allingham watercolour. Even minor roads in England today are bands of dark grey tarmac. But a white road is as poignant a memory of my childhood as cowslips, kingfishers, scarecrows, collecting pinecones in a go-cart, stirring pigwash in a tub, finding heartsease and corncockle in the cornfields, or filling jamjars with tiny frogs in a stream.

A white road was a rough thing to fall on, and country children always seemed to have grazed knees and bandages which stuck to the wounds. I am not sure how old I was when my brother John had a mild epileptic attack and fell heavily on a white road, and the accident was my fault – I was probably about fourteen, and John would have been twelve, but he was already very tall, ending up at six foot two. We had gone for a long country walk in Berkshire, and when walking with John on any surface harder than grass one was meant to hold his arm to support him if he should have a 'turn' and lose consciousness for a few seconds – a form of epilepsy known as *petit mal*, which developed into *grand mal* when he grew up. I was not strong enough to hold him up single-handed, but one could break his fall, so that usually not much harm was done. But on that occasion I had grown weary of walking arm-in-arm and become careless, probably stopping to pick flowers, and he had fallen face forward on the white road and hurt himself terribly. His face was cut all over and streaming with blood, but he was, as always, stoical about the pain.

I was thoroughly frightened, for in those days it might be hours before a car came by, and there was no cottage in sight, but miracles do happen. After a few minutes sitting by the roadside, a car came along *and we knew the driver*. He collected us and drove us to a doctor, who mopped up the blood and put a stitch in poor John's nose.

The calamity was magnified for me by the awful guilt I felt, for I had failed in my duty. I was also apprehensive that my parents might see the casualty before the bruises and cuts were healed, and I would be in trouble, though John, always my loyal and devoted friend, would make light of the accident. I marvel now that two children should have been allowed to wander alone through thinly inhabited country, but I think that in those days it was pretty safe, and though we had misadventures, we were never molested. The white roads were crude, but they led through magical country to favourite destinations, such as the sweet shop where they sold paper packets of liquorice sticks dipped in fizzy sherbet.

Berkshire was not the only country where we took our solitary expeditions. It chanced one summer that we two were paying guests at a house in Llandudno – we had no previous connections with the town, but my father had been there on a journalistic assignment, accompanying his political hero, Lloyd George, when he was taken seriously ill with a burst appendix and had to remain in the local hospital for several weeks. While there he met a doctor who thought he might be able to improve John's condition with a new treatment, so as soon as the school summer holidays started my mother, who had been visiting my father in Llandudno every week, took us with her. When Daddy was better, he and my mother returned to London and we two children stayed on so that John could try the treatment, a course of injections with a new, though not in John's case successful, drug.

Llandudno itself had little attraction for us beyond a plentiful supply of ice-cream cornets, but we had begun to explore the glorious mountains of the Snowdon range with my parents, who would hire a cheap taxi for the day and take a picnic lunch. Except for a few overcrowded beauty spots, such as Bettws-y-Coed, where little old ladies in tall Welsh hats and red flannel petticoats popped out of picture-book cottages treating us to ingratiating curtseys and smiles, the entire region of north Wales seemed to us as wild as when George Borrow roamed it in the 1850s. We were all devouring his *Wild Wales*, admiring his infinite energy and curiosity, though my mother suggested that he must often have infuriated the natives by lecturing them on their own language and history. Not a modest man, he was not slow to correct their Welsh or put them right on matters of local customs.

When my parents went back to London, I had no intention of sticking to the town of Llandudno. I studied the country bus timetables, and two or three times a week John and I would take a bus to some remote village and set off walking, penetrating further into the mountains than we had been able to do with my parents, for my father was still convalescent. Though I admired the spectacular and much-painted Welsh scenery of peaks, gorges and fast streams rushing from waterfall to waterfall, it was the peaty, boggy lower slopes of the mountains which I liked best, where I might find wild flowers. Sometimes we would come across a blue lake scattered with waterlilies, and the stone walls still sprouted with late foxgloves. Usually we saw no living creatures but sheep, but occasionally there would be a shepherd's cottage where we could get tea or milk and bread and butter. These cottages were not much more than glorified stone-and-slate huts, with no enclosed gardens, and in the remoter valleys the cottagers spoke only Welsh. But the Welsh have a genius for communication and a long tradition of kindness to strangers which extended to two weary and scruffy children. It was difficult to persuade the shepherds' wives to accept a little money for our tea. Once we strayed much further than I intended, and we had to run down a sodden moor and scramble over stone walls without looking for gates or gaps to catch the last bus home. The bus fares were a mounting problem for me, for though my father had left us with generous pocket money, he had not dreamed of long-distance excursions.

I must have told many lies to our landlady as to where we had been. Indeed, I was always telling lies as a child since what I wanted to do, and meant to do, and did do, often failed to correspond with parental orders. As my Victorian father counted truthfulness above all other virtues, I must have caused him a lot of pain when found out, and I am deeply sorry for it. But the generation gap yawned wide after the first war, many parents being stuck in the rigid cement of Edwardian and Victorian values, and I thought my father hopelessly unenlightened. I grew truthful in due course, though when my parents tried to regulate my sex life when I was in my twenties, frankness was again in abeyance. I had either to shock my parents or deceive them, a dilemma which many grown-up children of old-fashioned parents have had to face.

Looking back, I think there was a fair amount of hypocrisy in the strait-laced standards they applied to their daughters. Did they never stray from the narrow path themselves?

The Cult of Cornwall

Before package travel brought the world to our doorstep, the English middle-class family spent its holidays in Britain, and every father had a 'special' English county towards which he felt possessive. He had discovered it long ago, he had private memories of it before the tourists swarmed, he still knew the places where these horrid people had not yet penetrated, he was eager to be his children's cicerone.

My father's county was Cornwall, always a beckoning goal for artists and intellectuals, to whom every other county seemed suburbia by comparison. He had gone to Cornwall with reading parties in his Oxford days, sometimes camping ('I will show you how to make a fire with damp sticks'), bathing in the Atlantic rollers ('you must plunge in and get your head wet at once'), catching mackerel from a fishing boat, reading Aristotle in the evenings. He wanted us to enjoy Cornwall as he had done, and to Cornwall we went nearly every August in the early 1920s for our family holiday. Daddy would take a few days off in the spring, pack a haversack, and go on a walking tour, usually in Cornwall, occasionally in Devon, and look for rooms for all the family in August, 'rooms' being lodgings in a small house or large cottage where meals and service were provided and no other guests were taken during our stay. They were usually clean and comfortable, more homelike than a hotel, and much cheaper.

Luckily, we children responded well to Cornwall and my mother was at her best there, at least in the first week of the holiday, until the monotony got her down. She could be wonderfully amusing when not distracted by home cares, ill-health or various phobias which included a terror of thunderstorms so intense that she would not only tremble and rush round the room when a storm was imminent or in progress, but would talk fearfully about thunderstorms all the year round. We soon grew to love Cornwall's jagged coast, the quiet coves with their silver floor of shells, the breakers crashing on the headlands, the unfamiliar flowers (fuchsias, hydrangeas, tamarisks), the mewing of sea birds, the limpets and starfish, the rich cream breakfasts and crab teas. But the curse of these holidays was the climate, and I cannot remember a single one when it did not rain for weeks on end – even in the drought year of 1921 August was remorselessly wet.

We would eat our picnics in the lee of a slimy breakwater, we would snatch icy morning bathes (we never swam for two hours after a meal) with my mother standing on the shore holding rough towels to envelop us when we emerged shivering and blue, ready with a thermos of cocoa and petit-beurre biscuits to restore our circulations. Even today, if one of my fingers goes dead, I think of Cornwall and get a whiff of wet bathing-suits and seaweed. Perhaps my weather memories are subjective, for it seemed always sunny in Berkshire, but search my memory as I will I cannot once recall toasting on a warm beach. Today, I and many of my friends feel as possessive about France as Daddy was about Cornwall. We knew the Dordogne, the Languedoc, Provence, the Camargue or the Loire valley when they were *French*, before package tourists came with their insatiable demands for chips and toilets. I am also, as you know, élitist about Greece, and thankful that I knew the lovely Peloponnese when it was lonely and undeveloped. Perhaps one day you will tell a younger generation, 'I knew Malaysia before it was wrecked'. The horizon moves ever farther away.

On our Cornish holidays we did not do much in the way of 'sightseeing' in the sense of visiting Cornish churches and historic houses, for Cornwall is really not that sort of county. The cliffs and coves and fishing villages with their steep cobbled streets of painted thatched cottages were the places we sought when we made our expeditions to Land's End and Kynance, Coverack and The Lizard. Also, our family tastes and opinions in my childhood were dominated by my father, who was above all a man of letters, and we were all more interested in books than architecture. However, he had inherited the Victorian addiction to 'scenery'. All through the nineteenth century romantic scenery had a vast aesthetic appeal, the craggier the better, and this in turn descended from the eighteenth-century discovery of Claude, Salvator Rosa and other painters of the picturesque. Switzerland was a goal for every Victorian traveller who could afford it, from athletic clergymen to young ladies with sketchbooks, though the Lake District, Derbyshire, Scotland, Wales or Cornwall were respectable substitutes, especially for honeymoon couples. This love of nature's grandeur was still strong in the first quarter of the twentieth century – even such cultured characters as Harold Nicolson and Vita Sackville-West, when they were in Persia, were happier in the mountains than among the mosques of Isfahan.

So in Cornwall we sought the starkest cliffs and the most frightening rocks on our long walks, and the pasties and splits we ate for lunch were usually soaked in spray. It was not until I went to Oxford and met friends whose choice was cathedrals rather than mountains that I began to care for antiquities and to have dreams of seeing Chartres or Rome.

My Cornish adventures did not end with my early childhood holidays. Later, in my St Paul's days, I spent an Easter week in Cornwall as the guest of a school-friend, Diana Hubback, whose mother owned a white, slate-roofed house on the cliffs overlooking Constantine Bay. Mrs Hubback was a prominent feminist and her adult guests were pillars of the suffragette movement, including that grand, formidable campaigner, Eleanor Rathbone, soon to be elected MP for the United Universities. Liberated people, we all bathed naked in the freezing April sea, much to my astonishment, for as children we were accustomed to seek the protection of sand-dunes or rocks when changing into our bathing costumes, my father modestly choosing a different dune or rock from that of my sister and myself. I was somewhat mortified to see what a beautiful figure Diana had, with genuine breasts, for I was skinny and flat-chested.

When I told her afterwards, my mother was convulsed with laughter to think of those large, serious, middle-aged ladies flopping about as ocean nymphs, and perhaps only Cornwall, ever hospitable to the artist, would have permitted such pagan behaviour. Nude bathing at Eastbourne would have brought out the police.

The Family Doctor

I will call him Dr M, even to you, because he has descendants still in medical practice. He was our family doctor through most of my childhood, when we lived in Bayswater and he in the neighbouring, but smarter, district of Notting Hill.

Everything about Dr M was substantial. His house was enormous, with a full domestic staff including a butler and maids in uniform. He himself was a tall, portly man who wore a black coat, striped trousers and a gold watch and chain. He owned a Daimler in which he was sometimes driven on his rounds by a chauffeur, though he more often walked. He was a pillar of the parish church. Mother liked him because he was 'so safe', unlike his predecessor, a clever but volatile character whom my father dismissed when he made amorous advances to my mother. We liked him because, though awe-inspiring, not to say pompous, he was kindly and invited us to his children's parties, which were lavish, with lovely food, balloons, dancing and games, and a magic lantern show or a conjuror. Mother called him 'Dr M' and he called her 'Mrs Scott-James'; there were no Christian names in those days, or matey conversation.

When Dr M came to visit us, preparations were made as though we were receiving royalty. The invalid's room was washed and polished, the maid warned to have a kettle of water on the boil, to put out clean towels, and to hover near the front door so that the doctor should not be kept waiting for a second. Not that Dr M was ever in a hurry; he seemed to have infinite time. As there were three of us children, all subject to the usual infectious diseases, and as Mother was often unwell, we made frequent requests for a visit and he always arrived within an hour or two. He invariably came to our house; I do not remember ever going to his consulting-room. The frenetic timetable of the modern private GP, dashing from sickbed to sickbed in the morning and dealing with a steady flow of appointments at the evening surgery, 'the relentless treadmill of family practice', did not exist for Dr M, who took on as many patients as he wanted and no more. He did not attend our living-in servant, for she was 'on the panel', a primitive version of the National Health Service, and had a different doctor who was paid by the state, but he was equally conscientious and though she normally joined the queue at his surgery, he visited if she was seriously ill. Perhaps it was the golden age of family health.

Dr M was a cautious doctor, not given to new-fangled drugs or treatments, but at least his prescriptions were of his own devising and were made up individually by the chemist. He did more than just select from a catalogue of proprietory pills. If one of us had a mysterious temperature or stomach-ache his diagnosis was usually, 'There's a lot of it about', but he was very good on spots. Measles, German measles or chicken-pox were identified at once and we were put to bed for a good long illness. He insisted on a bedroom heated by a coal fire, and as my room had only a gas fire, when I caught measles, whooping-cough, or some other of the childish ailments which we all had to suffer before the advent of inoculations, then available only for smallpox, I was transferred downstairs to my father's study. Here there was a coal fire which my father would stoke when he came home late at night from his newspaper, throwing on first a bucket of slack and then a jug of water to damp it down, so that it kept in all night. I enjoyed these removals, for my father's study was lined with books which I read secretly, though how much I understood of *The Return of the Native* or Matthew Arnold's *Essays in Criticism* is doubtful. I also loved the flickering flames of the fire, and the first dish of food which was brought to me when I was well enough to 'take solids'. It was always steamed plaice on the first day and on the next my favourite chicken, which was a luxury in my youth before merciless factory farming made chicken cheap.

Convalescence under Dr M was a slow affair. One was prescribed a 'tonic', usually containing iron, and there was none of that dashing back to school or the office which today's patient attempts as soon as the temperature drops to normal. You could pretty well reckon a term off for an infectious disease. As quarantine was strictly observed in most schools, so that perfectly healthy children who had been in contact with an infection were sent home for weeks, it is a miracle that one got educated at all. The modern theory is to 'throw them all together and let them get it over before they are adults', which is probably sound, especially in the case of German measles, which carries dangers for pregnant women, and mumps, which is said to render grown men impotent, though perhaps this is a myth.

Occasionally Dr M would send one of us to a specialist, joining us in Harley Street for the appointment, but if the case was serious, the specialist came to the house and, in the case of a surgeon, operated there. My appendix was taken out on the kitchen table, which was moved into the dining-room for the purpose, and I clearly remember the horrible smell of the chloroform mask, and the still more horrible jokey remarks with which the surgeon and anaesthetist tried to cheer me up, the nurse chiming in with, 'She was a brick about the enema' before I mercifully went under.

I don't remember Dr M ever changing in any particular. His treatments remained traditional and his appearance formal – he would never have visited patients wearing a lounge suit. He was reticent about a patient's condition, not given to frank discussion about the Heath Robinson machinery of the human body, which he regarded as his province, not ours. He oozed self-confidence, which I like in a doctor. Some years ago I was four thousand miles from home in America's middle west when I developed a burning rash which I took to the local physician. He said, 'It could be anything. Travel fatigue. A food allergy. Reaction to vaccination. I'll give you a prescription which may or may not clear it up. Good luck.' I was dismayed. I wanted him to *pretend* to know. I like a GP to be a wise old bird, like Trollope's Dr Thorne, for instance, a father figure to be respected, as we all respected Dr M.

Oxford Gloom

In 1931 I went up to Somerville College, Oxford, in a cloud of foolish hopes which were never realized. I don't know quite what I expected, but certainly a much more sophisticated society than I found, including brilliant conversation and a heterosexual social life. Disillusionment was swift. Suddenly, after the freedom and wide interests of life in London, I found myself an adult at a boarding-school with convent rules designed to discourage easy friendship between men and women. The men undergraduates, anyway, despised us, having just left their public schools and come up together in friendly clumps. 'Keep away. You are not wanted here. We are all friends, men content together. We want no female to trouble us,' wrote Rosamond Lehmann, who had been to Cambridge, in *Dusty Answer*. 'The whole point of Oxford is that there are no girls,' said Compton Mackenzie's priggish hero, Michael Fane, in *Sinister Street*, who devoted himself to manly friendships at the university and to reforming fallen women when he went down. Even if not 'content together', it was still *fashionable* in my time for young men to herd with their peers. If some precocious young man did want to be seen around with a girl, the last one he would choose would be an undergraduate; his aim would be an actress, preferably a musical comedy star.

Oxford was a good place for female swots with their minds concentrated on their degrees, and doubtless a good place for lesbians, although I never consciously met any. And it was a tolerable place for the few who broke all the rules and led a heady mixed social life of whom I (wrongly, but my façade was well constructed) was held to be a front runner. For the others, it could be a lonely world, with every twinge of melancholy aggravated by the rain-washed spires, the tolling bells, and the miasmas from the river. Oxford always seemed like some wonderful party to which one had not been invited.

I do not know to what extent Oxford was homosexual at that time; certainly John Betjeman, writing of the previous decade, said 'everyone was queer at Oxford in those days', though Betjeman's wild generalizations must always be taken with salt;

and Noel Annan, in *Our Age*, claims that homosexuality was a cult with 'all the thrill of the illicit', but admits that 'in the end most of the participants got married, soon after going down'. Certainly the prevalence, at all periods up to the war, of bachelor dons living in college tended to create all-male cliques, and I must admit that higher education was still so new for women that it tended to attract clever freaks – most female undergraduates were ill-dressed and unattractive. But often attitudes changed for both men and women after a year or so at the university as they shook off the inhibitions of their schooldays and became more worldly.

My first year was certainly the worst, and even today Oxford girls have told me that their first year was distressing. They talk a lot about 'pressures'. My second year was much better, for I had met more people. It was the custom at the women's colleges for college tutors and older undergraduates to give sherry or coffee parties for the newcomers which could be a springboard for friendship with both men and women, and slowly my circle grew. (Please note the word 'undergraduate'. The word 'student', with its probably unmerited implications of public rebellion and private scruff was unknown at Oxford.) At one such party I met an undergraduate in his third year at Balliol and we fell in love almost at first sight. We spent every possible minute together, and talked of marriage, and the intercollege messenger system must have groaned under the weight of our love letters. But when he went down in my first summer, we drifted apart. I had two other proposals of marriage during my time at Oxford, one from an intense young historian who suffered from spots, one from a Rugby blue in the medical school, both of which I turned down with a callous contempt which makes me shudder with remorse to remember. At eighteen one meets emotions in others which are new and unexpected and one may deal with them crassly, not understanding their depth. I remember *laughing* at the Rugby blue, but luckily he did not grieve for long.

Though I had enough friends in my second year to keep loneliness at bay, I found the university social regulations idiotic and annoying. If I was invited to a college dance or stayed out after 10.30 p.m. at something as innocent as coffee after a concert or cinema, I had to climb over the Somerville wall to get in, being hoisted up by my escort and dreading a drop down the other side into the arms of some strolling don. Visiting a friend at a man's college, I had to sneak furtively up the staircase to his rooms hoping that the college porter would look the other way. It was all so silly. Another social disappointment was that I never found the brilliant conversation I had hoped for. Invited to a glittering dinner party by the classical historian, Alan Blakeway, who was attempting to teach me ancient history, I was surprised that all the talk was Oxford gossip. Have you heard the latest about Maurice Bowra? Who was Dick Crossman off with now? Nothing seemed to have changed much since the days of Edward Gibbon, who wrote that the fellows' conversation 'stagnated in a round of college business, Tory politics, personal associations, and private scandal'.

Of course there were compensations. There was abundant music at Oxford; many of my friends played in amateur orchestras and I sang in the Oxford Bach choir. (Music, part of the fabric of life at St Paul's, was positively discouraged by my Somerville tutor as a distraction from work.) In the summer there was tennis, and one of my tutors, a don at Worcester who, being happily married, was not terrified of women, gave Sunday tennis parties at his home in north Oxford to which I would bicycle with my friend Kathleen Timpson, later Ollerenshaw, a mathematical genius and now a DBE. But the greatest compensation of all was Greek.

Greek is a beautiful language to the ear, the eye and the mind. It is acknowledged to express ideas with unique clarity, but I think its charm has been underestimated. The pathos of the return of Ulysses to Ithaca, the kindness of Nausicaa and her family in Phaeacia, the wicked fascination of Alcibiades, are revealed as perfectly in Greek as are the laws of logic or oratory. Greek, and Latin to a lesser extent, raised a loving appreciation in me which has proved lasting. They also brought out my competitive spirit. Most of us women had never had our brains tested in competition with men – lamenting at our evening coffee parties that we were an inferior sex, we doubted if we would ever have won a place at a men's college – and I was anxious to prove myself to myself by getting a first in Honour Mods, the exam which comes after five terms of a classics course and covers Greek and Latin languages and literature. Men and women take this exam on equal terms. So for two years I read for Honour Mods, at first lackadaisically, more seriously towards the end, and got my first with room to spare in the spring of 1933.

After that I read Greats for one horrible term, Greats being largely philosophy, a subject which bores me to the point of stupor, for I am a worldly person, loving people and places and art, but never happy wandering about in a maze of abstract ideas. My father kept telling me that philosophy enlarges the mind, but I chose to keep mine small, or perhaps already had inklings that there were other ways of growing up mentally.

To complete my course and take a degree I would have to spend two more years reading an uncongenial subject when I was longing for London and a job, and I left the university in June 1933 in a storm of college and parental protest. I think I must call Oxford a period of academic success, as far as it went, which was half-way, but personal failure, for I never managed to appreciate what is to so many a Promised Land.

Wide-eyed in Europe

Today every twenty-year-old seems to have been to Kathmandu. It must be the Blackpool of the East. I don't know how their parents can afford it, but the young, and not only the rich, expect to 'take a year off' to see the world either before or after university or between school and the first job. Lucky for them, not always so lucky for the host countries.

My own earlier travels were rare and brief, but were treasured all the more for their scarcity value. Money was tight at home, I had family responsibilities, and once in a job my holiday time was exiguous. In my first job, which I was to land some six months after leaving Oxford, I was given one week unpaid in the first year, one week paid and one unpaid in the second, and I think three paid weeks thereafter, though I am not quite sure. By pre-war standards, this was not ungenerous.

I had only twice been out of England as a child, when our seaside holiday was spent in northern France instead of Cornwall, once at Wimereux, a dull resort near Boulogne, and once at the much prettier Villerville, in Normandy, but I must have been small, for my memories are misty. The only visual image which sticks in my mind like a postcard in an album is of the Rue du Gros-Horloge in Rouen, where a massive and richly decorated renaissance clock bestrides a medieval street of half-timbered houses, the earliest of my recollections of architecture. I think we went to Rouen from Villerville for the day. I did not see the great clock again until 1988, when I went on a five-day tour of Normandy cathedrals with the Folio Society, and there was the clock in all its grandeur in the heart of Old Rouen, and, far from feeling old and sad, I felt again the wonder of a child. Rouen was heavily bombed in the last war and has been much restored, but well. The French are not afraid of copying the antique in appropriate places – the great square at Arras, largely destroyed in the first war, is another example – and for me restoration in traditional style often works better than filling in the gaps in an ancient street with 'relevant' slabs of concrete.

I remember, too, quite clearly, on this Normandy holiday, the

French family picnics on the beaches, so superior to our simple sandwich lunches eaten sitting on our beach towels. Theirs were elaborate affairs with tables and chairs and china plates and wine and a host of dishes, even, I fancy, hot ones. The whole family, from the *grandmères* to the tots, would be dressed in resort rather than beach clothes, for the French preferred strolling on the promenades to dipping in the chilly sea. The ladies wore shady hats and carried striped parasols and (I reflect with hindsight) might have been descendants of the elegant ladies and gentlemen painted by Boudin, Sickert, Jacques-Emile Blanche, or some other of the many French and English artists of the nineteenth century who were charmed by the watering-places of Normandy and their delightful social life.

My first adult excursion abroad was in the long vacation after leaving Oxford in 1933, when I went on a three-week outing to Czechoslovakia, and the sense of wonder is with me still. I went across Europe by car with some Oxford friends, Sally Graves and Richard Chilver, whom Sally later married, and we had a rendezvous with more Oxford friends in Prague.

Travelling by road, you savour to the full the relationship between your point of departure and your destination. A plane takes you 'bong' from London to Rome, Cairo or Tokyo, and there is nowhere in between, no geography, no history, no art, no people, just a tip-back seat and a plastic tray. But along the road from London to Prague there is a necklace of antiquities, landscapes, local customs, changing languages, varied food. Probably bicycles or feet would bring you into even closer contact with the countries *en route* than a car, but we had not the long weeks to spare. The only hitch in our plans was that we had no car. This was solved by a trip to the Euston Road, the centre of the used-car trade, where we bought an old crock for £100 on the understanding that the dealer would give us back £90 if we returned it in good condition. Amazingly, he did, which was lucky for me, who had with difficulty raised my share of the price.

Of the three, I was by far the most naive traveller. Sally, in particular, had spent much time abroad as her father, Philip Graves, had been a foreign correspondent of *The Times*, and she spoke good German, of which I knew not a word. She and Richard were amused by my inexperience, and even today I am shocked at how little I knew about architecture. My background was literary; to aesthetic marvels I had unopened eyes. Driving across Germany, stopping at such splendid towns as Würzburg and Bamberg, I had my first conscious sight of baroque, which I had scarcely heard of. Brought up on Gothic as the accepted style, I was half dazzled, half appalled at the extravagance of the churches and palaces of southern Germany, every inch of their vast interiors decorated with stucco and gold leaf, scrolls and garlands, paintings and carvings, with lascivious cherubs and irreligious-looking angels filling every scrap of space. The public taste for baroque was still fairly new, and Sacheverell Sitwell wrote in his book *German Baroque* in 1927 that there was no previous book on the subject in the English language. Nor had I yet made serious acquaintance with Romanesque, let alone Byzantine, art. I knew a little about Greek and Roman architecture and sculpture, though I had not seen so much as a column or a bust outside books and museums. Of the treasures of England I was still painfully ignorant, for so many of my holidays had been rural, my absorbing interest being wild flowers.

A less pleasant discovery in Germany was the all-pervasiveness of the Nazi menace. In a small village in Bavaria a horrible old man spat at Sally and myself in the street, calling us lipsticked whores. Not all the political columns in the English newspapers had taught me so much about Nazi beastliness as that small, unattractive incident. It was with a sense of relief that we crossed the frontier from Bavaria into Czechoslovakia, not yet invaded, still gloriously free.

We drove to Prague through southern Bohemia, formerly a reluctant province of the Austrian empire, and the experience was a joy. The country is a rolling plateau with mountain peaks a few thousand feet high, and in the clear, crisp air (now, I believe, heavy with pollution), one always felt hungry and well. There were fine churches and castles which we stopped to visit, but we chose mostly the minor country roads which meandered through a chequered agricultural landscape of meadows and streams and fields of corn and vegetables, with dark patches of pine forest and slate-coloured lakes. One had to drive slowly through the villages which teemed with honking geese. You will laugh when I tell you that one novelty to my modest eyes was the sight of sunburnt men working in the fields stripped to the waist, for in the thirties a shirt and possibly a waistcoat discreetly covered every farm labourer's chest in England.

We often found our beds for the night in farmhouses, where we were kindly welcomed and charged next to nothing, and we fed very well on goose, eggs, vegetables and fruit, with coffee and bread for breakfast. At inns and cafés on the way Richard and Sally drank Czech beer, but I (I know you never believe this) drank nothing but water until I was forty, when Fleet Street tempted me to gin-and-tonic. Once we were reduced to straw beds in a barn, but slept well.

When we arrived in Prague all our friends had turned up and we met at the time and place appointed, and our little party spent two days sightseeing in that tragic but beautiful city of domes and spires and winding medieval streets. Then Richard, Sally and I continued in our crock with the intention of driving to Poland, but we did not get so far, turning for home when the country grew bleaker and the pine forests solid and monotonous.

Since then I have travelled far and wide, sometimes (when paid for) in luxury, sometimes on the cheap, but few journeys have given me more pleasure than that first foreign encounter with no social obligations or business appointments, just unplanned days and companions who were always in a good humour. I knew that this would be my last carefree outing for a long time, for the serious business of job-hunting awaited me on my return to London. I felt an obligation to be self-supporting as soon as possible for I had left Oxford against my parents' wishes, and there, having a Somerville scholarship and a leaving exhibition from St Paul's, I had cost them nothing. But they did not rub it in, or try to rush me into something unsuitable.

Job Hunting

It is only now, in the 1990s, when the Thatcher bubble has burst and left a trail of economic misery, that you can have an idea of what it was like to be jobless in the 1930s. I know there have been industrial depressions in your lifetime, but the professions did not suffer deeply, certainly not in London, and for several decades after the war any competent woman looking for a first chance could find one. At times there has even been over-employment, jobs chasing people, so that a clever woman could pick and choose.

The autumn of 1933 was a rock-bottom time to be unemployed, and it took me six months to get my first permanent job. In the interval I worked hard answering advertisements in the newspapers, following up as many introductions as my parents could give me, and going for interviews. By the end of the year I knew something about brick walls.

In the thirties, whatever your potential, women were still regarded as a low form of working life. They were paid less than men for the same work and fewer avenues were open to them. There were jobs for women in teaching, nursing, journalism, fashion, decorating and design, a few women broke into advertising, and there was always secretarial work, but women were rare birds in politics, the City, at the bar or in the higher ranks of the civil service; they had a hard time getting places in a medical school, and were shut out of the business boardroom. There were no women judges, ambassadors, newspaper editors, or captains of industry. I am not writing a feminist tract – indeed, I am only a half-hearted feminist – but I wanted to give you a sketch of the job possibilities when I was young. Noel Annan in *Our Age* wrote, 'One half of our age found few ladders to climb. They were the women … in the upper classes it was still thought unusual for a girl to want a job let alone excel in a profession.'

One of my first interviews was granted me in all kindness by a friend of my parents who was a director of the famous biscuit firm, Huntley & Palmer. He gave it to me straight.

'We do not employ women, Anne, except at factory level, and we have no present intention of doing so. One of my bright young nieces had her eye on the firm, and I told her the same thing. Women aren't good at business, and it wouldn't be fair on the men.'

Was there not even the humblest opening in an office?

'No, only in the factory, and that leads nowhere. Your mother tells me you went to Oxford. Frankly, that's a disadvantage. There is no room in industry for educated women, the men don't like them.'

My next interview, also with an introduction, was with a firm of high-class wholesale dress manufacturers. Yes, there might be an opening for a 'matcher', a girl who would go round the shops with small pieces of fabric buying sewing silks to match. I think the pay was about £1 a week, and I did not pursue this dead-end occupation.

I answered any promising advertisement including one for a bright, educated girl to help with correspondence on Weldon's, a working-class women's magazine. I was summoned, went along, was accepted on trial, and sent home with a supply of stationery and a bundle of readers' letters to answer at home – a large batch of perhaps, a hundred letters, for there was a backlog. They made pathetic reading. Most were ill-spelt and badly expressed, pitiful because the poor women felt a false confidence that some omniscient stranger at Weldon's would lighten their burdens with wise advice. The commonest practical problems were how to make a smart new dress out of a dowdy old one and how to clear up persistent facial spots, but these were far outnumbered by the anxieties of the lovelorn. There were girls with reluctant boyfriends, wives with errant husbands, many simple creatures who asked, 'He goes out a lot with another girl and does not answer my letters, do you think he really loves me?' One woman wondered, more mundanely, why her cakes fell flat.

I should, I think, have sorted the letters into piles and worked out a few standard replies which would fit all but the stickiest cases. But I felt so sorry for the writers that I answered each letter conscientiously and at length. I remember to this day writing to one girl who was going to a dance and had only a short, twenties-style evening dress and no prospect of affording a new one. I suggested that she make a gathered overskirt of net, short in front and dipping at the back, and I drew a sketch. I sometimes wondered if she made the overskirt and what it looked like, but perhaps she only wrote the letter because she felt lonely, and anyway, the letter had been lying around Weldon's office for so many weeks that the dance must have been long over. I rang up our doctor to ask what I should write to another girl who had frightful monthly periods, and he said she should go to a doctor at once and if they were as bad as she said there wasn't a minute to lose.

It took me three solid weeks to wipe off the backlog of those letters, typing my replies on Weldon's writing paper. I then took them into the office to be posted, was thanked and given twenty-five shillings pay. I wasn't desperate enough to work for this pittance, so I said goodbye to my career as an agony aunt.

In reply to another advertisement I was shortlisted for a job which seemed to offer a living wage and genuine prospects. It was with Lewis's store in Liverpool, but I did not get it. The high-powered interviewer may have seen through my protestations that Liverpool was the only place where I wanted to live.

In November I landed a temporary job at Harrods, who were taking on selling staff for the Christmas season, but I continued to answer advertisements and struck gold at last, and started my first real job, in the New Year of 1934. I stayed in it for seven years and will tell you all about it.

Dear Old Harrods

When I worked my Christmas stint at Harrods, it was not, of course, under an Arab hegemony, but was a national institution like the Bank of England or the Athenaeum. Today, when you enter Harrods you are warned that closed-circuit television will catch you if you try shop-lifting, and you once told me that you were barred from entering by a commissionaire for wearing a dress revealing two inches of bare midriff.

In my time, though there was a discreet system of detection, the store gave the customer a friendly welcome. Many comforts, now banished upstairs, were available on the ground floor. Here the weary customer could relax in a deep leather armchair in the lounge, obtain cash from the bank or deposit heavy shopping at the Parcels Office. Though the Food Halls downstairs were already legendary, upstairs there was food for the mind in the form of a first-class lending library. When this was closed a few years ago, the last fig-leaf was blown away, leaving commercialism naked.

If Harrods was an institution, so were its customers. There was a 'Harrods type of customer', recognized by the staff at a glance, mostly women of the well-heeled upper middle class who entered the shop to buy, not to wander, and had charge accounts. They always wore hats, and fur coats in the winter, and their expressions were self-confident, not to say commanding. The Scott-Jameses, I must tell you, were not the Harrods type; we shopped at Barkers.

My temporary job at Harrods was selling toys at their Christmas Toy Fair. As you know, I have always loved having a job and can't think how all you young ones can endure the risks of freelancing, even if you make more money. I like the security of a job, but even more the buzz of an office, the fellowship of working with the same colleagues every day, the pleasure of always finding somebody free for lunch at short notice, the technical facilities, the regular pay packets and the career structure. Though I work now as hard as I ever did, I lead the lonely life of a writer, and I miss the news and gossip. There was plenty of both at Harrods.

Harrods at that time was strong on good staff relations, almost paternalistic and I thoroughly enjoyed it, though I was not a great success, for I cannot sell hard. Thrifty myself, I did not like to see customers overspending, and I remember saying to one lady, 'Harrods is much too expensive for Christmas stocking toys, you want Woolworths', and telling the millionaire Edward Hulton, who wanted to buy an enormous rocking horse for a child of two (possibly his nephew Jocelyn Stevens, who would not thank me for down-rating his horse), 'You should get the smaller size.'

I observed with wonder how the experienced staff could sell people toys at ten times the price they had intended to pay. Dear little old rosy-cheeked Miss Edgell, who had long retired from Harrods, but returned for every Toy Fair, was in charge of soft toys, and under her seemingly gentle, but in fact steely, persuasiveness, a customer who had come in for a small bunny would end up buying plush teddies, pussies, piggies, elephants, giraffes, and half the cuddly creatures of the animal world. Similarly, the man in charge of train sets would send a male customer who was thinking in terms of a circle of track, an engine and a signal, out of the Toy Fair carrying Clapham Junction.

Oddly enough (a tycoon friend has told me this), people who sell well are easily sold themselves, and conversely, people who cannot sell are sales-resistant, and it is quite difficult to sell me a pup, or even something of good value, because I always say, 'I'll think about it.' This same tycoon, himself a crack salesman, told me that if another high-powered salesman came to see him, he had to be protected by more hard-headed members of his staff from making rash deals, such was the buoyancy of his nature. I did get a little better at selling toys as the season advanced, but not much.

My social life as a salesgirl at Harrods was wholly agreeable. At first, the regular staff looked warily, even resentfully, at the 'temps', regarding us as pin-money girls. There was also a feeling among the male staff, bred by the depression, that it was unfair for a woman to work at all. A job was a man's prerogative. 'Unless a woman is a widow, or her husband is unemployed, she should stay at home.' But when they saw that I clocked in punctually and tried hard to learn, they melted, and sometimes an assistant would ask me to join him or her for the tea-break. The Harrods staff restaurant was excellent, and though I usually nipped out for lunch to get a change of air, I could get crumpets and honey in my tea break for a minuscule sum. In spite of the low prices, some of the married men would have a cup of tea only, every penny being important, and if I was sitting with them, I would order the same. One soon learned which of the men were under financial stress, which of the single women had mothers to keep, and, of course, which of the younger girls were having unhappy love affairs. Happy love affairs seemed scarce.

After Christmas there was a difficult week when customers poured back with complaints or parcels of broken toys – 'My poor little daughter cried herself to sleep when the stitches came apart and the stuffing fell out' – and as far as I remember everything was replaced unless the claim was obviously fraudulent or the children had treated their new toys with exceptional violence. After that, I did a week in the Coat Department during the January sale, which was no fun at all, for the shoppers were not 'the Harrods type', but fat, cross women trying to squeeze themselves into coats too small or too fashionable for their dumpy shapes. Soon after that I got the permanent job I needed, a job with prospects, but I always remember the old Harrods, a shop which I rarely enter now, with affection.

The Real Thing

Like Peter Fleming's *Brazilian Adventure*, it started with an advertisement in the agony column of *The Times*. *Vogue* magazine was looking for a girl who would double up as assistant to both the Managing Director, Mr Harry Yoxall, and the Knitting Editor, Mrs Haskett-Smith. I applied and was summoned for an interview with Mr Yoxall.

I overdressed for the interview, putting on an outrageously bright tartan suit which my mother and I had thought was just right for *Vogue* (I would have done better in a little black dress) and a choker of huge wooden beads. I arrived at the Bond Street offices half an hour early and walked the streets with fluttering bowels until my appointment was due. In those days there was no elaborate employment network of management consultants, head hunters, CVs and all the rest of the appointments system, which was to arrive soon from America. Getting a job depended partly on experience and partly on personality, and the interview, not the application form, was the important way in. If an employer liked you and thought you had potential, he gave you the job, otherwise not. (The interviews at Oxford and Cambridge colleges, rather than the computer, often decided the award of scholarships in the same way.)

Mr Yoxall was a tall, heavy, dyspeptic-looking man in his late thirties with a deliberately intimidating manner, though I learned over the years that he was a brilliant executive and scrupulously fair, and I had immense respect for him. Boss of an office with a high quota of hysterical women and epicene men, he acted as a sort of policeman, as well as being policy and financial chief, though subject to our American proprietors, the famous magazine publishing house of Condé Nast. (He later became a JP and was much sought after as a masterly chairman of publishing councils and committees.)

He asked me some penetrating questions and discouraged me by saying that I was young for the job (I was still only twenty) and might find it difficult to acquire a sense of chic – that tartan suit was nearly my undoing – adding that *Vogue* was a citadel of 'gracious living', whereas I had no experience of fashion, beauty, décor or entertaining. I felt untidy, ignorant and gauche.

However, unlike the previous employers I had seen, Mr Yoxall was in favour of educated women – he was a Balliol man himself – and thought enough of me to take me into the adjoining office to be looked over by two of his staff. One was his personal assistant, whose place I would fill if taken on, as she was leaving with a brave ambition to go to China, the other was the Knitting Editor, a new arrival, Chris Haskett-Smith. We four had an unexpectedly jovial conversation, in the course of which I assured Chris that I was an experienced knitter, a necessary qualification, and she must have signalled her approval, for when we returned to his office, Mr Yoxall glared at me sternly, but said he would offer me the job on a month's trial, the salary to be £3 a week for that month, and £3 15*s*. if I was retained. 'Your work will be split in two. You will act as general dogsbody to me in my capacity as publicity chief, and to Mrs Haskett-Smith as Knitting Editor. My work gets priority.' On enquiring further, I found that the publicity work would consist mostly of writing copy promoting *Vogue*, and preparing the illustrated 'house-ads' which appeared in every issue announcing the treats to be enjoyed in the next. This did not daunt me, but I wished I had not been so boastful about my knitting skills. I think I had told them that I could knit anything from a pair of socks to a tailored suit, whereas garter-stitch squares for a charity blanket were my highest achievement to date; but never mind, I had several days in which to practise, and I bought a nice booklet called *First Steps to Stylish Knitting* on my way home.

A week later I was sitting at my first office desk, sharing a large room with Chris, who was to be a friend of mine through many vicissitudes until her death some twenty-five years later. Mr Yoxall's office was next door, but the terror of his proximity was relieved by Chris's genial personality – she was a great life-enhancer who took *Vogue*'s alarming ideals lightly and found the pursuit of gracious living thoroughly entertaining. She was what is best described as 'a good sort', a retired army officer's wife with an experienced, weather-beaten face, who had lived for years in India when her husband's regiment was stationed there. They had met in France during the first war, where Victor was in the trenches and Chris was driving an ambulance, and they had fallen in love and married as soon as possible. At the same period Chris, whose convictions were instinctive rather than theological, became a Roman Catholic, on the grounds that the Catholic priests were braver at the front than the C. of E. padres, and I don't think her religion went deeper than that. She had given birth to two sons in India, but one had died and she told me that in those unhygienic days the loss of a child in an Anglo-Indian family was all too common.

On my first day at the office, Chris greeted me with, 'I'm afraid we've got another parcel.' She had a heap of knitted garments on her desk and held up a grotesque jacket with one long sleeve and one short one, and seven buttons but only three buttonholes. She handed me a very angry letter from a *Vogue Knitting Book* reader who had been following a *Vogue* pattern, and explained that she had arrived at the office only a month before I did to find a major cock-up in the Knitting Department. *Vogue* had bought the translation rights of some French knitting books and had published the instructions without checking them, unaware that French knitters are so clever that they do not expect line-by-line instructions, but make them up as they go along. Chris of course altered this system for the future, but meanwhile frightful garments were coming into the office by every post, and Chris felt it was our duty to put them right. She herself started on the offending jacket and handed me a dear little baby's pullover with no hole for the head and told me to reknit it. I then had to confess my ignorance, so she showed me how to unravel the garment and make headroom for the baby, and I was soon reknitting all manner of misfits under her tuition. Mr Yoxall would treat himself to a rare smile whenever he came in and gave me some copy to write and saw us groaning over our work. I preferred copywriting to knitting, and used every excuse to put my needles aside. When the faulty knitting book went out of print the angry parcels slacked off, and I enjoyed helping Chris with the next knitting book, and she even allowed me to design a simple sweater.

I stayed with *Vogue* for nearly seven years, though in time I graduated to more exciting duties than knitting. I moved over to the editorial department, first as a sub-editor, writing copy and captions and commissioning articles, and later I was made Beauty Editor, when my friend Mollie Fordham left to join the *News Chronicle* and I took her place, and was given a room and a secretary of my own. The work involved writing regular beauty features for *Vogue*, but also editing the *Vogue Beauty Book* which came out twice a year as a supplement tied to *Vogue*. On one glorious occasion I edited an issue of *House & Garden*, also a tied-in supplement, when for some reason it lacked a regular editor.

Vogue was quite an informal office and the staff was tiny compared with the battalions which are there today, and as *Vogue* was then a fortnightly magazine, and is now a monthly, I sometimes wonder what they all do. I think there must be stricter demarcation rules today, every employee having his or her own slot or title, for I remember doing a bit of everything myself, especially in a crisis. Also, much more time is spent today at business parties, furthering the aims of marketing and public relations, about which we knew little.

I wasn't a journalist – yet – but I was half-way there.

Learning the Trade

Careers moved slowly in the thirties and you were expected to learn your trade. I don't think there were any teenage newspaper columnists fresh from college, or directors of publishing houses in their twenties, or yuppies in the City, and few business tycoons who had made a pile, lost it, and made another pile before they were forty. Even in show business the great names were oldish people, like Cochran, Hitchcock, Lilian Baylis. I make no judgement on this reverence for experience rather than fresh thinking, which lasted until youth burst its banks after the war. Much young talent and enthusiasm were certainly lost. On the other hand, for a young career man or woman there was a certain satisfaction in the slow, steady climb. It was at least less risky.

I must have worked for Mr Yoxall for about three years before he handed me over to *Vogue*'s editorial department, and in those years he trained me himself. In spite of his high position, he taught me how to write copy, send it to press, organize the illustrations and read the proofs, and took trouble with every word I wrote – advertising copy has to be exact and succinct; the copywriter cannot wander. He also taught me the basics of layout and typography. There was of course a lot of publicity material which I did not write myself – some of it came from America and had to be adapted – and by the time he passed me on I was a pretty good sub-editor. After a year or two, Mr Yoxall began to consult as well as direct me, and though not lavish with praise he gave me a general feeling that I was giving satisfaction. Note, dear child, that I still refer to him as Mr Yoxall, for it was five years before he suggested that the staff should call him Harry, and this was at the prompting of our American bosses, who found the manners of the English office somewhat formal. Christian names, and their implications of office democracy, came to England much later. There was no, 'Well, John, and how does it feel be Prime Minister?', or, 'For an appointment call Marilyn on 001234.'

I still regard sub-editing as the nuts and bolts of journalism. Had you, dear child, at the age of twenty or so, announced an intention of following your father, mother, brother, two grandfathers and one grandmother into journalism, I would have advised you to learn sub-editing at the outset. If you can write copy quickly and concisely, can fit the words into the space, chop or add a line or two without ruining the sense, proof-read and choose a typeface, you are much better equipped as a journalist than the master of prose who has never learned his journalistic ABC. Outsiders, however successful as novelists, academics or politicians, tend to write fifty per cent more words than they were asked for and then feel insulted when their masterpieces have been 'butchered', as they call the cutting process. Looking forward in time to my days in Fleet Street I will defend newspaper subs to the death. On *Express* newspapers in their heyday, where technical standards were superb, I have cabled copy home from abroad, where I could not keep an eye on its fate, and found it so carefully cut that I could not find the holes. That is sensitive handling by a man in a sweaty shirt working in a hot noisy room against the clock.

When I moved from publicity to editorial, I had some new linguistic rules to learn. *Vogue*'s style of writing was quaint by Fleet Street standards; it was excessively sprightly and riddled with clichés: 'pencil-slim', 'nostalgic', 'vibrant with colour', 'spiced with white' rolled off the pen. It was hortatory, instructing the reader to 'take stock of yourself', 're-think your dinner parties', or 'look in the mirror and see what you can take off'. The punctuation was peculiar, with a generous sprinkling of colons, dots and dashes, even the occasional exclamation mark. But given its eccentricity, the standard was meticulous. The rules of *Vogue* layout demanded that every last line of a paragraph must be more than half a line, that the final line on a page must be a full line, and that the headline must exactly fill the space allotted by the layout men without one letter over or under. And *Vogue*'s sub-editors would have shuddered at the modern computerized way of dividing a word which runs over from one line to the next without regard to etymology. I am shocked today when the stately *Times* or *Telegraph* prints 'q-uestionable' or 'so-domy'. (No wonder children spell badly with such examples.) The sub-editors also had to shape the scrappy notes sent in by the fashion editors into coherent copy, and to do it quickly, because every press day was an Olympic sprint. I learnt sub-editing in a strict school and loved it, as I do to this day. My heart lifts at the sight of a batch of proofs and I rush for my pen.

As I have told you, I was involved on *Vogue* at various times with the beauty industry and with decoration, but I never had much to do with the fashion side, which is of course *Vogue*'s *raison-d'être*, and with my casual style of dressing, flat shoes and aversion to hats, I never looked like a fashion editor. But I learned how to transform thoughts quickly into print.

Private Lives

Some two years after I joined *Vogue* my salary reached £5 a week, and, as I was earning about £1 extra writing copy for an advertising agency, I felt I could afford a flat of my own. My parents protested only feebly, for my sister had paved the way and, facing appalling rows, had taken her own flat years earlier, and I found a one-room flat in a new block just off the King's Road in Chelsea, with an alcove where the bed could be curtained off, and a modern kitchenette and tiled bathroom, which seemed to me like the Ritz. The King's Road was still a romantic place where artists and writers gathered, with real bakers and greengrocers where the rubbish shops now blare forth pop music and sell dusty T-shirts. My rent was £90 a year, quite a lot out of my income, but as central heating and hot water were included I managed quite comfortably. When my salary later rose to £6 I could also afford a car, and I bought a secondhand Morris Cowley.

I loved that flat and stayed there until I married in 1939. I basked in its privacy. At last I was free from the inquisitions of my parents and could come and go as I wished and entertain whom I pleased without criticism. Like many very tall people, I am not by nature gregarious and I never had jet-set tastes, so my life in Meriden Court was enjoyable but far from flashy. I had a small circle of close friends, some dating from Oxford days, particularly Richard and Sally Chilver, others whom I knew through *Vogue*, such as Chris Haskett-Smith and *Vogue*'s ravishingly pretty receptionist, Mary Horsman, who later became godmother to my son, and I to hers. My Oxford friends had mostly gone into the civil service or were academics (Sally ended up as Principal of Lady Margaret Hall, Oxford); one or two were in publishing. *Vogue* friends included a few painters and illustrators. We were all young professional people and none had a lot of money – we had not at that time a country house or weekend cottage between us. Sometimes I was mildly in love, sometimes not. I was a fairly dedicated career girl, and as I wanted to write, and there was no opportunity for writing on *Vogue*, I knew that one day I must leave the security of a job I fully understood and move on.

One great pleasure most of us shared was occasional weekends driving into the country, searching out the loveliest villages and scenery, staying in an inn or farmhouse, and walking and sightseeing until it was time to drive home late on Sunday evening. The Cotswolds were a favourite destination, but sometimes we went as far as Devonshire or Wales. Another recreation was music and I went to concerts, especially the proms at the Queens Hall, where we stood for two or three back-breaking hours to save the price of a seat; I also collected records for my HMV portable gramophone, Bach then, rather than Mozart, being the composer beloved by the serious-minded young. Once in a way somebody rose to giving a small dinner party, perhaps for a birthday, but none of us was a good cook. We never thought of nightclubs. On solitary evenings, if I wasn't playing records, I would make pots of tea and read late into the night, some books for pleasure (Evelyn Waugh, Graham Greene, Agatha Christie, Hardy, Stendhal, Flaubert, Tolstoy, American novels), some only because it was the thing to do (Aldous Huxley, the Sitwells, James Joyce, Virginia Woolf); sometimes I would keep my hand in at Greek or Latin. I bitterly blame myself because I did not spend some of my plentiful free time going to modern language classes. I still know no German, and only tourist's Italian. Not long ago when reserving rooms by telephone for myself and a friend at Arezzo I asked not for two rooms, but for two waiters.

And there was the cinema.

It is impossible to overestimate the importance of the cinema to my generation. I went at least twice a week (on Saturdays all seats were a shilling for the noon performance at the local fleapit) often taking my brother John, and soaked in celluloid emotions from the *c'est-la-vie* melancholy of French films to the happy-ever-after optimism of Hollywood. I would sit rapt while Gary Cooper and Jean Arthur, Clark Gable and Claudette Colbert, Fred and Ginger, the men all romantic idealists, the girls all virgins, went through an hour and a half of misunderstandings until truth triumphed in the last reel and the couple united at the altar.

Of course I was not deceived by this simple view of life. I was a sophisticated character and knew that most of the plots were cheapish and some of the acting pure ham (and I would not exempt Garbo). But the films of the thirties were so superbly produced, so dazzling, so *enjoyable*, that I do not regret the hours I spent sitting in my red plush seat. Such was their charm that later generations have rushed to every revival. How many times have you revelled in Busby Berkeley?

Though most films were no more emotionally moving than eating chocolates, there were also some fine movies, even masterpieces, with memorable acting, which I never missed. Emil Jannings in *The Blue Angel*, the Marx Brothers, many French films such as *La Femme du Boulanger* or *Hotel du Nord* were classics by any standard, and I think one could include William Powell and Myrna Loy in *The Thin Man*.

One deprivation which I regret, but it couldn't be helped, was that I had few opportunities for foreign travel. Holidays were shorter and it took longer to get far away. As I will tell you, I went once to New York before the war, and twice I went to France with friends, which was cheap, beautiful and so unexploited as to be almost medieval. One of us would produce a car and we would travel slowly across country in pursuit of food, architecture, and the French way of life, enjoying Roman ruins among the olive groves of the south, or Romanesque churches among the many streams of the Dordogne. The food was lovingly cooked everywhere, uncorrupted by the microwave or *nouvelle cuisine*, and we would study menu after menu in some cobbled square, always written in purple ink, before deciding which establishment to enter. 'This one has *fraises des bois* for a *supplément*.' 'Yes, but the other had them on the three-course menu.'

Those early holidays were brief, but there was a freedom and spaciousness and sense of well-being about them which I do not forget.

The Camera and the Brush

If I gave you a copy of *Vogue* in the thirties you would scarcely recognize it, for the fashion pages looked quite different. To your eyes the photography would seem stilted and old-fashioned, and most of it was in black-and-white. On the other hand I think you would appreciate the first-rate fashion drawing which gave variety and sparkle to *Vogue*'s pages. In those days, there were artists of wit and imagination, often gifted in other fields, such as theatre design, most of them working in Paris, who enjoyed drawing fashion for *Vogue* and *Harper's Bazaar*, particularly covers. We had a small quota of colour pages which were usually allotted to these graphic artists, for colour photography, at least in England (it was making strides in America) was still crude.

But most of the pages were photographic, and the style of photography was highly artificial. The unreal was always preferred to the real, the vision much influenced by Hollywood. Just as a Hollywood director making a film about Cleopatra would build the pyramids and the sphinx in California and import a few crocodiles rather than shoot his film in Egypt, so most of *Vogue*'s photographs were taken in the studio rather than on location. The backgrounds devised by the photographers were of Babylonian luxury, and the ideal was glamour.

Glamour, a dated word today, was a Hollywood invention. It was the aura diffused by every famous film goddess, by Garbo, Dietrich, Hedy Lamarr or Myrna Loy, it was the setting of the spectacular movies of Paramount and Metro-Goldwyn-Mayer. Glamour implies not only beauty, but also wealth, and *Vogue*'s sitters, whether society women or professional models, had to look *rich*. Furred, bejewelled, masked in make-up, set among silks and satins, gilding and flowers, the sitter posed under intense lighting for a photographer who used a plate camera and slow film, so that the pose had to be held for several seconds or the picture was blurred. These long time-exposures required immobility, the body held stiff and the face blank, but in a china-doll way the sitters did look lovely. Their beauty was much enhanced by heavy retouching of the negatives, every flaw in the complexion painted out, every bulge in the body tactfully smoothed away. Horst, André Durst, Cecil Beaton, Erwin Blumenfeld, were pre-eminent among the photographers of this wondrous never-never-land, Horst the finest of them, doing work of enduring quality, and Beaton a lightweight by comparison.

A recurring element in the fashion photography of the thirties was surrealism, not surprising in the heyday of Salvador Dali. Cecil Beaton often abandoned his usual tinsel backgrounds and turned to surrealism, with its sinister undertones, photographing the dancer Tilly Losch entrapped in coils of paper, or models standing in empty corridors among broken columns symbolic of decay. I myself once worked with Blumenfeld, a brilliant German, to produce a surrealist photograph which was considered a triumph. I was then *Vogue*'s Beauty Editor, and I needed a picture of a beautiful face to illustrate an article on skin care. Blumenfeld had elected to take the model, a fine-boned blonde with an exquisite nose called Cora van Millingen, in profile, smelling a long-stemmed rose. In the studio he changed his mind, and sent me out to buy a swansdown powder-puff, and when I returned he snapped the rose from the stalk and pinned the powder-puff in its place for Cora to sniff with an expression of ecstasy. It sounds silly, but it was enchanting.

This static fashion photography lasted almost up to the war, but a livelier style began to emerge towards the end of the decade, under the influence of the picture-news magazines which were winning huge circulations in other countries. In Germany there were the famous news magazines, *Berliner Illustrierte* and *Münchener Illustrierte*, which were to inspire our own *Picture Post*. In the United States there was the bombshell of *Life*, launched by Henry Luce in 1936, which enormously impressed *Vogue*'s American proprietor, Condé Nast. It persuaded him that his fashion magazines must be more journalistic, with more reporting, more interviews, more realism and more pace.

The photographers, especially the younger ones, responded, snapping their models in action – natural girls now, not dummies, with lighter make-up and flying hair. Increasingly they abandoned studio backgrounds in favour of real locations, moors and mountains, markets and mean streets. I was intensely attracted by this newsier kind of photography, and when Edward Hulton's *Picture Post* burst on London in 1938 I felt an instant longing to work for it, but with no reporting experience, no by-lines to my credit, no friends in Fleet Street as opposed to Bond Street, I never thought I had a chance.

The other medium of fashion illustration, that of painting or drawing, had reached its peak in the 1920s, but it was still highly respected in the thirties. It declined during the war, never to revive, to me a deplorable loss. Its greatest contribution in its heyday was to magazine covers.

In the early twenties, *Vogue* cover drawings were not just faces, but complete pictures. The artist was an illustrator, drawing scenes of fashionable life – an exquisite couple at the opera, an idealized country lady in faultless tweeds striding the moors with her thoroughbred dogs. Georges Lepape was prominent among these masters of commercial art, his figures elongated, his colours flat, clearly influenced by Modigliani. In the late twenties, Eduardo Benito started drawing covers of faces only, without the bodies, stark, remorselessly modern close-ups which owed nothing to the older arts of illustration. By my time in the thirties the style of drawing had changed again, and, led by Carl Erickson (Eric), and followed by Christian Bérard, fashion drawing became fluid and calligraphic, owing more to Lautrec than Modigliani. Sometimes *Vogue* was able to commission Raoul Dufy to paint one of his joyous scenes – I remember a Dufy cover of the *beau monde* disporting itself at the races. All these artists except, I think, Dufy, drew inside pages as well as covers for *Vogue* and, breaking into the catalogue of photographic pages, they gave style and change of pace.

I wish we could see covers of such distinction on the bookstalls today, but magazine editors tell you that drawings on the cover 'don't sell'. Apparently readers want, month after month, the *same* cover – a close-up colour photograph of a vapid face – and all the magazines, up-market and down-market alike, carry almost identical pictures. Why, I ask, buy *Vogue* rather than any other? I suppose the circulation managers know their business, but I feel in my bones that one day good fashion drawing will come back.

The author, aged three, with her sister, Marie, aged ten, in the garden of a house in Aldermaston, Berkshire.

Above: *in the St Paul's tennis team, looking smug in the centre back row.*

Opposite: *Cecil Beaton took this picture in the thirties for* Vogue, *but it was not used, so he gave it to the author as a compensation.*

Rose Cottage in its doll's-house days. It was enlarged later.

Cecil Beaton's Finest Hour

One of the historic milestones of the thirties was the Coronation of King George VI which *Vogue* felt was a special challenge to the magazine as an arbiter of high society. King George was to be crowned on the 12 May 1937, and for many weeks in advance *Vogue* was in a ferment planning a special Coronation Number. This duly appeared on 28 April, a blockbuster of 210 pages, rich in advertising, but it was not an artistic success. This was partly because any Gala Number of any publication tends to strive for decorative effect at the expense of content, and the result is all gauze and tinsel.

At that time, royalty was a notoriously difficult subject for the press to cover. A line had to be drawn somewhere between the iconoclastic and the unctuous. Serious writers did not care for royalty-mongering unless the subject was far enough away in the past to be history and artists didn't want to paint royal personages unless they could be granted a sitting, a privilege usually reserved in the 1930s for Royal Academicians. The remoteness of the Royal Family in that pre-Fergie period, the quasi-religious awe in which it was held, can scarcely be imagined today, the aloofness of King George VI and Queen Elizabeth being even more marked than that of George V and Queen Mary to compensate for the débâcle of the Duke of Windsor – the shattered myth had to be restored. So *Vogue* had quite a problem.

American *Vogue* was as enthusiastic as we were about the Coronation, and was prepared to pay well for material, so we had more money to spend than usual. We approached top writers and artists for royal contributions; nearly all agreed to take part, nearly all fell down on the job. The one exception was Cecil Beaton.

Unfortunately for me, *Vogue*'s hard-pressed editor picked on me to help her to commission and oversee the contributions, and I did not do well. I first asked Rex Whistler to draw three family groups of the Royal Family in what we hoped would be a Winterhalter manner, but it was a mistaken choice, his style being too rococo for so earnest a subject. There was to be one group of the King and Queen with the young princesses, another of Queen Mary with the Princess Royal and the Duke of Windsor, another of the Gloucesters and Kents. (There was considerable heartsearching as to whether or not the Duke of Windsor should be included.) Poor Rex found every line a struggle and ran alarmingly behind schedule. I went to see him every week to collect anything remotely finished and to put some moral stuffing into him, and would find him looking painfully young and vulnerable, sitting with his head in his hands, saying, 'I hate it, I hate it, can't I be let off?' The 'Winterhalters', drawn of necessity from photographs, were indeed a disaster, bad likenesses of chocolate-box insipidity, not improved by touches of pink on the cheeks and dresses. The Princesses looked like wax dolls, the Duke of Windsor like an advertisement for hair-cream. Nobody was happy, least of all Rex Whistler, but the space was allotted and the drawings had to be used.

My next conspicuous failure was with Vanessa Bell, whom I had asked to paint a needlework design on a royal theme. Surprisingly, she agreed, for the Bloomsbury set, of which she was a founder member, was accustomed to pillory the monarchy, and she designed and painted a jewelled crown on a velvet cushion, the whole framed in Tudor roses. What could be better? But again, the royal subject seemed to inhibit this accomplished artist, and the design was feeble. I had arranged for stamped canvas patterns to be made up for readers to purchase and embroider, but the demand was small.

Other contributors were not, thank heaven, approached by me, and some did better, but not much. Sacheverell Sitwell produced an elegant piece of word-spinning about family life, coaches, regimental uniforms and so on. Raymond Mortimer wrote an essay about nothing. Oliver Messel painted a colour fantasia of a costume ball which entirely lacked the magic of his sets for the theatre. The only contributor who really enjoyed himself, because snobbery was a word he did not understand or dread, was Cecil Beaton, whose assignment was an eight-page gallery of photographs called *Beauties of the Day*.

Cecil himself, a born impresario, and our society editor, a racy American bachelor from the Syrie Maugham world, arranged sittings in our studio for five duchesses (Buccleuch, Richmond and Gordon, Westminster, Marlborough and Sutherland), two marchionesses (Carisbrooke and Anglesey), a countess (Pembroke), three viscountesses (Wimborne, Castlereagh and Weymouth), with Lady Louis Mountbatten, Lady Nunburnholme, Lady Diana Cooper and Lady Brownlow thrown in for good measure. The excitement through the office before the sittings was intense, and we all craned our necks to catch a glimpse of the highborn or at least well-connected beauties before the studio doors closed behind them. Each was photographed in front of rich draped curtains, and satins and brocades, taffetas and velvets, were imported into the studio by the bolt to be draped and tasselled by Cecil's minions, along with baroque furniture and cartloads of flowers from Constance Spry. All the beauties were magnificently dressed and wore their tiaras. All behaved well, or so the studio secretary told me afterwards, such was Cecil Beaton's magnetism. The Gallery of Beauties was the big success of our Coronation Number, for we had visibly penetrated the upper echelons of society, and *Vogue*'s honour was saved. I must admit that looking back at those photographs, they look to me merely meretricious. Beaton's success on this occasion was not artistic, but in getting the job done at all.

It was a relief when our royal number was over and we could return to the business we understood of reporting fashion, beauty, house decoration and the theatre, the euphoria somewhat damped by blasts from New York about the poor material we had sent them, always excepting the Beaton portraits. Our American editors could not understand why we had not achieved exclusive interviews with the King and Queen, with perhaps a word or two from Queen Mary, and a special message to *Vogue* from the Archbishop of Canterbury. Nor could they see why their own all-American Duchess of Windsor was left out of the Gallery of Beauties. The mystique of royalty in the pre-war world was beyond their ken. Today, when royalty competes for media favours, often with results disastrous to its own dignity, indeed to its very survival, *Vogue*'s task would be immeasurably easier.

Brilliant New York

All through my *Vogue* years the influence which dominated our magazine was New York. New York led the world in magazines in the 1930s, so much so that when some bright spirits launched *Night and Day* in London in 1937, it was a slavish copy of the *New Yorker*.

New York was at its brilliant peak in the thirties. The depression was passing, the self-doubt and iconoclasm of the post-war years was far in the future. Manhattan was a dynamo of feverish excitement, with its theatres and nightclubs, its stunning architecture, its beautiful, extravagant women, its cynical wisecracks, its enormous cars and its sparkling magazines. New York exported new styles and manners to London, from Elizabeth Arden cosmetics to Syrie Maugham's white sofas and armchairs. London food took on a New York flavour, with new breakfasts of orange juice, cereal and black coffee and new salads with fruit and nuts mixed in with the lettuce and dressing. Waffles, sweetcorn and lemon chiffon pie were newcomers to snackbar menus.

British *Vogue* was owned, as you know, by the American publisher Condé Nast, and was a humble offshoot of the New York edition, from which we drew many of our best features. American *Vogue* was rich and we were poor, and it supported us financially, largely through the fat profits of *Vogue* paper patterns, which were a thriving American industry. True, many of *Vogue*'s most gifted artists and photographers lived in Paris, which never lost its supremacy in dress fashion, but New York *Vogue* was their impresario and paymaster, and British *Vogue* was grateful to pick up the British rights to use their work. I think Cecil Beaton was the only English *Vogue* contributor whom our American editors regarded as an international star. Otherwise, they patronized us, were friendly but unrelenting critics of our efforts and bombarded us with uncomplimentary cables. At one stage, deploring our old-fashioned typography and layouts, they sent over an American art editor to buck us up. He was disagreeably surprised at the small resources available to him, being accustomed to an army of assistants to do the donkey work, which in London he had to do himself.

Once or twice a year, senior New York editors came to London on their way to Paris, and it shook up our complacency to see them at work. They were twice as energetic as we were, always alert for the original idea or the new name, and they did not clock off mentally when the office closed. Their job was their whole life, and their personal friends were their office colleagues. However charming they were socially, in business they were brutally frank. Once, the New York editor-in-chief, the formidable Edna Woolman Chase, came over herself with an entourage of secretaries and assistants, and, holding a series of conferences, she did not mince her words, for Americans at work don't waste time with euphemisms. Mrs Chase would never say, 'I'm sorry, this copy isn't tight enough', but 'Who wrote this nonsense?' She would criticize senior staff in front of junior staff, even, on one embarrassing occasion, rubbishing Mr Yoxall himself, but he accepted it bravely as a useful lesson in office democracy. When Mrs Chase left for Paris, we all felt relieved, but stimulated, pleased to be roused from our British lethargy.

Of course, being young and eager, I longed to go to New York, and when some American friends invited me to stay with them in 1935, I grabbed the chance. But would Mr Yoxall allow me the time? I had fourteen days holiday due to me, or sixteen with a weekend tacked on, and I needed eighteen days to fit in with the only possible sailing dates – out on the SS *Bremen*, a German liner, and home on the *Queen Mary*. Office holiday rules were strict, but I screwed up my courage and asked Mr Yoxall for two extra days, and with a characteristic 'Don't do it again', he said yes, and I booked my second-class berths.

New York made a child of me. From the moment when the Manhattan skyline hit me in the eyes, I was under a spell. Everything seemed bigger, better, faster, more beautiful than at home. Sailing into the skyline was itself an adventure. The skyscrapers, many built early in the century, with their wonderful decorative tops, peaked or towered, bulbous or Gothic, borrowed the architecture of many countries and centuries to make a city which looked more mythical than real.

My arrival brought me back to earth, with rude immigration men and hostile customs officers, but once through the barrier and hugging my friends, the magic returned. Everything seemed outsize. I thought I had never seen so many lovely girls, heard such witty conversation, known such sizzling heat, ridden in such grand cars, been dazzled by such rich merchandise, nor been welcomed by such huge flowers (peonies) in my bedroom. Even the ubiquitous black people were figures from a story-book, for the multi-racial society had not arrived in Britain. There were fewer than ten thousand black people here in 1939, and most country people had never seen a black face.

I visited *Vogue*, where the staff were cordial, small fry though I was, for Harry Yoxall had written about me in advance; some asked me to lunch and I was given tickets for the theatre. Condé Nast himself promised to give me a job if I wanted to return for a longer stay. Of French stock, he was very pro-European, and beneficent to his French and British emloyees. Had I gone to work there I doubt if I would have made a success of it, so fierce is the competition, a woman's career demanding a total dedication which overrides personal loyalties and occupations and is distasteful to me.

Of course I knew perfectly well that I was seeing only the materialistic side of New York, but why not? I was young and excitable and had come for a holiday, not as a social observer. I loved the pace, the bright lights, the instant service, the late nights in a city which never went to sleep, and the exhilarating ocean air, and I cried all the way home.

I was lucky to see New York at perhaps the most amusing time in its history. It is by nature a city of extravagance, and now that it is poor and run-down, much of the magic has gone. Even its physical beauty has diminished, for the elegant old skyscrapers are dwarfed by degenerate monoliths, featureless slabs of building crammed into every possible space to the point of suffocation. The collapse of the American dream was mercilessly exposed a few years ago by Tom Wolfe in *The Bonfire of the Vanities*, which took the city as its anti-hero.

I was lucky, too, to have the entrée to American *Vogue*, which enjoyed success and prestige. I believe that its prosperity faltered for a while after the war, but it recovered. Today, American glossy magazines still generate ideas and are technically accomplished, but the stunts and promotions outweigh the editorial substance, and they seem more razzmatazz than journalism.

Lesley Blanch

I cannot move on from my apprenticeship at *Vogue* without telling you about one of the most gifted and charming women I ever met, Lesley Blanch. I wish you knew her, but she has lived for a long time in France. Like Chris Haskett-Smith, Lesley was not a '*Vogue* type'. She was a bohemian, a nomad, an artist, deeply romantic, widely travelled, a spirited writer and caricaturist and a brilliant *raconteuse*. Her friends were theatre directors, actors, painters, writers, and many in the arts world, and she wrote *Vogue*'s regular arts feature called 'Spotlight'. She was allowed more freedom for her maverick opinions than any other staff contributor and took full advantage of it. Contributing to a series on cooks by well-known hostesses – 'My Cook is a Russian', 'My Cook is a Hungarian', and so on – she entitled her article 'My Cook is a Catastrophe'.

Lesley looked like a baroque angel. She had (still has) an oval face framed in a halo of honey-gold curls, a rounded figure, an expression of experience combined with innocence, if you see what I mean, as though she had taken many knocks in life, but they had not sullied her. Lesley had a feverish manner of talking, extravagant in praise of friends, vitriolic about enemies, and she lived in a whirl of melodrama – something as trivial as a missed bus became a black tragedy. She wore exotic clothes of Russian ballet inspiration and moved in a nimbus of veiling, often topped with a fur shako, to the accompanying music of jangling bracelets. She had the sweetest of smiles. She never seemed to have a penny. She was devoted to cats and burst into a storm of tears when told by a skin doctor that she had a cat allergy. Her favourite country was Russia, and she claimed to have visited its remotest districts with a Russian admirer at some unspecified time in the past. Siberia, Samarkand, the Caucasus were as familiar to her as Piccadilly or Chelsea.

I had not been long on *Vogue* when Lesley invited me to lunch at her flat. To my conventional eyes her living room was like a booth in an oriental souk. It was so crowded with furniture, Victoriana, books, plants, screens, shawls, china, pictures and photographs, candelabra, Russian icons and

Moroccan lamps, lustres and embroidered cushions that there was no obvious place to sit down. But like everything about Lesley, it had charm, goodness she had charm. And from the turmoil of her kitchen she produced an exquisite lunch, which we ate off flowered plates at a papier-mâché table with a crochet cloth (Lesley's own handiwork). She regaled me not only with good food, but with breathtaking anecdotes of her travels, her friends, her love life (heady), her feelings as an artist and writer. I felt a plodding pedestrian, which I was, in the company of one who travelled through life on wings.

A few years later, in the war, I lived with Lesley for a time when I was bombed out and homeless, and she had a spare room in a flat in a steel-and-concrete block in Chelsea, where she had somehow managed to transform her soulless bed-sitter into a stage set.

When she left the flat to get married to Romain Gary, a pilot in the Free French Air Force who later became a celebrated novelist and diplomatist, it lost all the personality she had given it. I was still living there when I married your father, and we continued there until Max was born, but after Nannie joined us the squash became too tight for comfort, and by the time you arrived we had moved to larger quarters in Rutland Gate.

It was not until after the war that Lesley's career reached its deserved fulfilment with the publication in 1954 of her romantic book, *The Wilder Shores of Love*, biographies of four nineteenth-century women who deserted Europe for the mountains and deserts of the mysterious east, an instant bestseller which fulfilled the fantasies of many a frustrated housewife in England and the United States. Just before it came out I wrote a feature about Lesley for the *Sunday Express*, for which I was writing a weekly column, accompanied by a photograph which exactly caught her intelligent beauty and quizzical glance. She claimed that two days later the newspaper was being used as wrapping at her fishmonger's. 'It was bizarre to see my kippers wrapped up in my face.'

Lesley's marriage was stormy, and given the characters of both husband and wife, brilliant but absorbed by their different careers, Lesley excitable by nature, Romain, a Slav by birth, usually steeped in gloom, a clash was inevitable, and they eventually parted. Romain later married the American actress Jean Seberg, and at different times both he and Jean committed suicide. Theirs was a deeply tragic story. I used to visit them sometimes when they lived in Paris, for which Lesley never forgave me. She felt that Romain should be ostracized by her friends, but I could not myself see the divorce in her unrelenting terms of black and white.

I last saw her at some time in the 1970s when I was married to Osbert, and we were staying with friends in the picturesque hill village of Roquebrune in the south of France. She had a ravishing little house there, almost a cave, which she had filled with Russian, Arab, French and Victorian furniture, knick-knacks and draperies, and with her usual profusion of potted plants. My friends took us with them when invited to tea, and though she was delighted to renew an old acquaintance with Osbert, she was cool to me.

Uncle John

I think it is time for me to write something about your uncle John, for he was supremely important to me for the forty years of his life and I loved him with an almost maternal love. In return he was my staunchest ally.

Like many who are handicapped, John was stoical and courageous. His one wish was to live as normally as possible, and though it was risky even to leave him alone in a room – witness his many bruises and scars – the family agreed that a constant watch would be torture to him and as a child he was given as much freedom as possible in the house. However, there was always one of us with him outside in the street, and the Saturday walks in Kensington Gardens taken arm-in-arm by my father and myself with John in the middle were heartily disliked by all three. When John grew older, it was no longer a question of the family choosing his mode of life, for he insisted on going about on his own.

Until my schooldays were over I was constantly with him, except for an occasional week staying with my godparents or a school-friend. I looked after him at weekends (there was always a row when I wanted to play in a school tennis match. My mother would say, 'It isn't fair on John', and John would say 'Go, Anne, I implore you not to stay for me'), and took him to Berkshire for country holidays. But when I went to Oxford and later took a job such close contact wasn't possible. However, when, after a few years at *Vogue*, I had taken my Chelsea flat John would often join me on a Saturday or Sunday to spend the day and go to the cinema. He was pretty miserable at home, where the atmosphere was oppressive, and my flat was his bolthole.

Of course, London was not a good place for someone with his disability and at one time he had a job on a market garden in the country where he was more independent. But after a year the market gardener who employed him, and gave a great deal of time to helping him, and the couple with whom he lodged, found the responsibility too great and the job came to an end. Unfortunately, John went through periods of depression when he would be very silent and was not easy company, and he would let his work slide.

In 1937 my parents felt that they could afford a weekend cottage, for my mother had inherited some money. This was again in Berkshire, though near the downs, not in the pine-and-heather country which I had formerly known so well, and John went to live there, my mother spending most of her time in the country, joined by my father at weekends. Here a new life opened for him. Country people are undoubtedly kinder than Londoners, and many were anxious to make his life happier. The village dramatic society asked him to join them, coaching him in his bit parts and pulling him through the performances without disaster. He took on some gardening jobs in the village, which he did well, as he was handy and muscular. He bicycled everywhere (dangerous, but traffic on country lanes was still light), and went to Reading on his own every Saturday by bus to go to the cinema. More than once he was brought home by the police, but they never grumbled and seemed to think that helping the unfortunate was part of their job. Several times he ran away in a struggle for independence, but he could never achieve it for long. The saddest occasion of all was early in the war when he was missing for two days and the police could not trace him. Then a young army officer turned up at my mother's cottage in a car with John in tow and said to her, 'I'm afraid there has been some mistake.' John had gone to the recruiting office and tried to join up. He was apologetic and ashamed, but we all congratulated him on his attempt and tried to persuade him that he was contributing to the war effort by working on the land.

A few years later, when I was married to your father and we had our own Rose Cottage four miles from my mother's, came perhaps the best time in John's unhappy life. He took over my garden and worked alone there during the week, though neighbours would look in every day and chat, and Saturday and Sunday he usually spent with us. Your father, who was tolerant of odd people, took John in his stride and even Max seemed to like him. Nannie did not actively complain, and you were too young to be involved.

When John died at the age of forty, not from epilepsy but from lung cancer, I felt as though a vital prop had been snatched from me. Helping John was never a one-way traffic. If I was unhappy, it was John who sympathized. If I had a headache, it was John who made tea and brought it to my bedroom.

Long after the war, when my mother had died, I suggested to my father that we should take John to London and arrange for him to see the best possible specialist. He had been on the same drugs for many years, and medicine had been completely revolutionized. I was making plenty of money now and we could split the cost. He wholly agreed, and John did indeed go to London and went through all sorts of painful tests at the Maudsley Hospital and a new regime was prescribed, but he was no better than before, if anything, worse. I think that even today not much could be done for him, for there was physical damage to the brain, probably incurred at birth.

Recollecting the attitudes of other people to John, I feel that women are not only kinder, but braver, than men in the face of handicap. If John were taken ill without warning, all sorts of accidents could happen, from a mere broken cup of tea to a crash into the fireplace, but women never seemed bothered by the risks. Most men were pleasant enough, but tended to keep out of the way.

Rose Cottage

In August 1938 I jumped over the cliff and bought a permanent home, the cottage you have always known and loved. It came about almost by accident.

I was staying at my parents' cottage in Berkshire and took my mother in the family car for an evening drive over the downs. (My father had learned to drive after a fashion, but my mother went white and shook with nerves before taking the wheel, and had mercifully given up.)

Returning by the village of Aldworth we stopped to look at the giant effigies in the church, and across the parsonage green I spotted a doll's house perched on top of a grassy bank with a board outside saying, 'Rose Cottage. For Sale by Auction.' I said, 'Oh, Mother, I wish I could have that', and we walked across the green and had a closer look. I had not a penny in the world for property buying and no thoughts of a home in the country, but sometimes, perhaps once in a lifetime, one responds so violently to a place that one feels impelled to live there.

We laughed it off, my mother and I, but I brooded about Rose Cottage and took Derek, my young man of that period, to see it, and he, too, fell under its spell. Mind you, it was not much of a place, just a small brick-and-tile cottage, two up and two down, with a neglected garden and no plumbing or electricity, the only source of water being a well. Two very old ladies had lived in it who died, as so often happens with close companions, within a month of each other.

When the auction date drew near my longing increased and I asked my mother if she would lend me some money. My father rightly thought the plan improvident, but my mother liked the idea of my living so near and agreed to lend me up to four hundred pounds to buy the cottage, and I bought it for exactly that sum, though I think I could have got it for less if I had been shrewder. The structure was fairly sound, but the inside was in a shocking state of disrepair and was infested with mice, woodlice and spiders.

I will not bore you with the banal story of how Derek and I struggled to put the place in order, nor of how badly I got into debt. These enterprises are all alike and we had our share of collapsed ceilings, fused electricity and sewage coming up in the sink. But I had to tell you about the discovery of Rose Cottage because it has always been deeply important to me, at first for its charm and later for its perfection as a modest family home.

When, a year after buying it, the war broke out and Derek joined the RAF, I rashly married him. The marriage lasted just a few months and later, when we were divorced, it was as though it had never happened. Neither of us seemed to feel anything at all. You cannot condemn me for my folly more than I condemn myself, my only excuse being that in that summer of 1939 there was a fair amount of false emotion in the air.

I must tell you how the cottage looked at that time, many years before I enlarged it to make room for Max, Nannie and you. It was square, like a miniature farmhouse, with a central path to the front door. The date has never been established, but I think it is late eighteenth century. In front was a small garden with old Arthur Rackham apple trees, bounded by a frightful mixed hedge which is still there and still frightful. (I ought to have grubbed it up at once and replanted with beech or box, but I had no cash.) Near the front door was a well, which we used as a refrigerator, keeping milk and butter cool in the hottest weather. Behind the house was a larger garden with more old apple trees, a nice old wooden shed and a derelict pigsty bedded down in solid chalk – the soil on that spot is still very high in lime.

The view from the cottage was worthy of Constable. We looked on to a triangular village green with a group of elm trees in the middle half hiding the fourteenth-century church. Just across the green was a pair of thatched cottages inhabited by two ancient men who never exchanged a word except to quarrel over the use of their shared pump. Their front doors would open simultaneously and they would pop out with buckets and have a row. Behind their cottages was pasture grazed by horses whose dung produced pearly, pink-lined mushrooms in late summer. In the distance was a farmhouse with a mighty barn, and beyond that a copse of wild cherry, so our view was wholly pastoral.

When the builders had left at last, I began to decorate Rose Cottage, and, working in the world of *Vogue* and *House & Garden*, I had seen the work of contemporary decorators, of whom the most gifted was John Fowler. His style, though individual, was nearer to Regency than any other period, and the stark, modernistic rooms of the twenties with their tweedy curtains and square Cotswold-designed armchairs were beginning to look dated.

The atmosphere John Fowler created was light, airy and elegant, with striped wallpapers against white paintwork, chintz-covered sofas, curtains with Regency drapes, Regency couches and gold-and-white painted chairs, and the bedrooms fluttered with white muslin. I was overwhelmed by the fresh beauty of Fowler's houses, gave up any idea of being original and adopted 'Vogue Regency' for the cottage. You have no idea how cheaply one could decorate and furnish before the war, for good pieces of secondhand furniture could be found for a few pounds. Having chosen red-and-white striped chintz for my living-room curtains, which I made myself, I bought a Regency couch for £5, a set of six Victorian dining-room chairs for £10, and (my most extravagant purchase) a painted dining_table from the Colefax and Fowler shop itself for £15. The cottage looked like a spring morning when I had finished it, and though it has been redecorated many times since, I have tried to keep the whiteness and feeling of fresh air.

Derek and I spent our weekends at Rose Cottage for a few months before we married and the war broke out, leaving all our lives in flux. Through the war I hung on to it by the skin of my teeth. Not only was it a luxury I could not possibly afford on my own, but when the blitz started I could not easily get there. So I let it for a year, and when the tenants mercifully moved out, I lent it to friends, two sisters, each with a young baby and a husband in the forces. In return for the cottage, they looked after the garden, which I was just beginning to plan and plant, and kept a room always ready for me if I could get away from London, when they would scratch up a meal. I usually arrived without notice, having walked three miles uphill from Goring & Streatley station carrying an attaché case and some food as a contribution to the pot. It will give you an idea of the stringency of petrol rationing when I tell you that the chances of getting a lift on the road were practically nil. There was almost no civilian traffic.

The husband of one of the sisters was a bomber pilot, and they had not been long at Rose Cottage before the dreadful news came that he had not returned from a mission over

Germany. Frances, his wife, reacted strangely. She rejected all sympathy and would not talk about her anxiety to anyone, even her sister. She was silent and cold, quietly doing her share of the cooking and housework, but taking no real interest in anything but her baby. She endured nearly a year of suspense, secretly cherishing a grain of hope, but then it was confirmed that her husband's aircraft had been shot down.

Early in 1944 the sisters decided to depart to their own homes, one in London, one in Kent, and I resumed possession of the cottage. In June of that year I married your father, then well-known as Macdonald Hastings, chief war correspondent of *Picture Post*, and we went to the cottage for our honeymoon, hoping for a quiet week. But we had not been there two days before the editor telephoned to say that the long expected Second Front had been opened and your father was whisked away to Normandy, from which he sent the brilliant despatches which you have read. Rose Cottage was put into mothballs again for a few months until the end of the war. But in my enthusiasm for the cottage I have run ahead of my story. I must take you back to 1940, and my challenging new job at *Picture Post*.

Picture Post

Picture Post was a visionary magazine in two senses. It reported the news through the eye – the eye of the camera. True, every feature was the creation of a team of two, the photographer and the writer, but the pictures mattered more than the words. In a deeper sense, *Picture Post* was visionary because it looked into the future as well as the present. It was a young, spirited and provocative magazine, political and reformist, and though it might claim to be non-party, its heart was with the poor, the unemployed, the wretchedly housed.

Though it had been created by the Hungarian Jewish refugee, Stefan Lorant, Lorant had just fled to America when I joined the staff and had been succeeded as editor by Tom Hopkinson. My appointment came about in this way.

As I have told you, I had admired *Picture Post* since its first issue and longed to work for it. In 1940 I bravely wrote out of the blue to the editor (Lorant) asking if he would consider publishing a feature about *Vogue* if our editors would agree. He said yes, and they said yes, *Picture Post* sent a photographer over several days, and I organized and wrote the story, which was published covering four pages. Soon afterwards Tom, who had taken over from Lorant, asked me to come and see him and said they were badly in need of a Women's Editor, having never had one, and would I like the job? I said yes, thank you, and broke it to Harry Yoxall, who was extremely upset and so was I, for I loved the whole organization at Condé Nast and felt I was leaving home, but it was a hothouse home, and it was more than time to face the world outside. After finishing my work in hand at *Vogue* and crying a bit at my goodbye party I went to *Picture Post* early in 1941.

Though Tom followed Lorant's principle of making every issue a mix of features of varying mood, from the blitz to the Windmill Girls, from the rough life of a deep-sea trawler to Tommy Handley and *ITMA*, he made the paper increasingly political and controversial, gradually building up a campaign for a more equal Britain after the war. In January, 1941, he devoted a whole number to 'A Plan for Britain', which provoked a huge response, and in succeeding years published many features demanding a new deal for the underdog which built up into a potent advocacy. Photographs could throw a searchlight on the stark facts of poverty in a way which only television, then in its infancy, can surpass today – a picture feature on a depressed coalmining valley in Wales was more persuasive than a score of newspaper articles or public speeches. But Tom did not forget that the magazine must also be amusing, and there was always the sparkle of girlie stories and sports features to relieve the sense of social mission.

The photographs in *Picture Post* were mostly what Tom called 'pictures by stealth', as opposed to the more old-fashioned 'pictures by consent'. The camera was the secret eye, catching people off-guard and life in its moments of truth, though I hasten to add that the bedroom intrusions of today's tabloids were not in its sights. Among various cameras used, the Leica was pre-eminent, small and inconspicuous, with thirty-six shots on a roll of 35-millimetre film which could be snapped at high speed and in various light conditions. When the great cockney photographer, Bert Hardy, covered the blazing fires of the blitz or when Leonard McCombe reported the Battle of Normandy, they would click like machine-guns.

Yet even so, a good photographer would be selective. There has been a lot of misunderstanding about the impromptu nature of news pictures. Even in an uncontrollable situation, such as a fire, the photographer can still choose the most dramatic moment or the most moving expression on a human face, while an insensitive photographer can cover an earthquake and make it look dull. In a controllable situation, from a children's party to a prison camp, it is never just a matter of pointing the camera and snapping. Scenes can be composed. Here it was the job of the journalist on *Picture Post* to help and direct the photographer, flattering celebrities, asking shy people to come forward, persuading a diffident family to give admittance to their home, chatting to children so that they forgot the camera and stopped smirking. The journalist was expected to subordinate his work to that of the photographer because he could check his facts afterwards or perhaps go back to the scene to complete his story, but the photographer must seize his moment or lose it for ever.

Where, you may well ask, did I fit into this fast-moving and politically conscious paper with the years on *Vogue* as my only training?

I was, as I have said, to be Women's Editor, but I knew that this was my chance to get away from purely feminine journalism. I could shape the job as I wished.

The war was already biting deep into women's lives. We had endured a harsh winter of the blitz, millions of women were in war jobs, while those looking after families at home were coping with shortages of every kind. Fashion would not rank high in my work programme, though even in the darkest days it was not negligible. The authorities discovered that a well-designed uniform attracted recruits to the services, factory managers that output increased when women had time off to get their hair done.

Tom gave me no lead at all as to how to run the women's features. He gave me an office and a secretary and told me to get on with it, and I had to learn by trial and error. I soon decided that most of my features must be of general, rather than purely female, interest, and that they must be linked to the news. So I produced week after week features on backyard farming, food preserving, women in factories, clubs for the troops, service wives, cooking with rations, childbirth in the blitz, new treatments for war neuroses, refurbishing a bombed home – there was no shortage of subjects in those days of change and challenge. Every feature had to be of pictorial value, and I found that bringing in celebrities would make a plain subject eyecatching. I asked Constance Spry, plump and motherly, with a humorous, Rembrandt sort of face, to let us photograph her working in her vegetable garden and cooking wonderful dishes with the produce. When in March 1942, the Board of Trade introduced Utility Clothes, with fabric-saving specifications, we photographed them on the beautiful new film star, Deborah Kerr. Pictures, pictures, pictures. You had to *see* every subject before you thought of the words.

I went through some fearful teething troubles. I mistakenly began by using photographers I had known on *Vogue*, but their pictures looked wooden in a news magazine, and I turned thankfully to *Picture Post*'s own cameramen. I went to my first interview without an idea in my head as to how to conduct it. It was with Dr Edith Summerskill, MP, and I am still embarrassed to recall that she had to tell me how to do it, she herself posing the questions and trotting out the answers. I had to learn the elements of the laws of libel, and that legal troubles always descend from an unexpected quarter. A calculated criticism of a person in the limelight will be read by the magazine's lawyers before publication, and therefore be reasonably safe, but some dim mother whose children you have photographed for a feature on family budgets, with whom you have spent much time and been on excellent terms, and to whom you have paid a fee for her trouble, will suddenly decide that little Johnnie or Emily has been seriously damaged by the publicity. (She has, of course, been prompted by outsiders who see money in it.)

Looking at life in terms of pictures soon became second nature to me. I have never had any ambition to use the camera myself, but I am a natural photographer's mate.

War Stories

One of the excitements of *Picture Post* was that my work took me frequently out of London. I am inquisitive by nature and knew that my knowledge of societies outside the small world of London publishing and fashion was painfully limited, and I loved exploring the provinces, meeting miners, farmers, servicemen, factory workers and their families.

One story which absorbed me took me to a hospital in the south of England (I think it was in Southampton, but for security reasons I was not allowed to locate it in my article, so have no record.) I had scraped acquaintance with the well-known psychiatrist, Dr William Sargant, who was a pioneer of new treatments for men with the war neuroses which were once called shellshock. He later wrote a classic book called *Battle for the Mind.*

Dr Sargant took me all over the hospital introducing me to men who had suffered various racking experiences which left them with severe psychological symptoms such as depression, anxiety, insomnia, nightmares, heart palpitations and loss of weight. He demonstrated some of the treatments, which fell into two classes, psychological and physical, though the two might be combined, as with deep sleep treatment, narco-analysis (in which the patient surrenders his personality and talks to the doctor under the influence of a narcotic), and the new method of electric shock treatment for depression. Some of these remedies left me morally uneasy, doubting the godlike status of a man who controls another's mind, though many, I know, were successful, for I followed up some of the cases in later months.

I am still haunted by the anxious face of a merchant seaman who had been torpedoed three times, and on the third occasion was flung into the sea with his best friend, who was drowned. The poor man was convinced that he could have saved his friend, and suffered depression and nightmares of the sea. After some weeks of narco-analysis he came to terms with his friend's death and knew that it was not his fault. He had in fact grabbed hold of him in the sea, but he slipped away.

I also remember a pathetic little bus conductor, a sensitive and conscientious man, who could not bear turning away queues of weary passengers because his bus was full. He became first depressed and then muddled, until he was no longer fit for work. After a course of psychological treatment he was able to return to a working life, though not as a bus conductor; he became a checker in a garage. Heaven knows how he would have been treated in the First World War, possibly as a criminal malingerer.

Another story in which I was participant as well as onlooker took me to Coventry and put me into the uniform of a bus conductress. I had arranged a series of features with the other women journalists on *Picture Post* for which we would each make a personal trial of a different war job – one agreed to take on the ATS, another to do a stint in a munitions factory – and I was to spend three days with the Midland Red Bus Company as a clippie. A photographer would accompany each of us.

I reported to the Midland Red office on arrival in Coventry, was given the address of my hostel, a navy blue uniform, with peaked cap and overcoat, and two hours' training, and told to report for duty the next morning at 6.10 a.m. I was to take the early shift in charge of Topsy, an experienced clippie.

I arrived on time, but tired, for I had had very little sleep. There had been an air raid warning in the night and a crump or two, and I discovered that a raid in a strange city is more unnerving than in one's own. I did not know what to do if the raid proved serious and I was too frightened to sleep. Coventry had suffered a severe raid the previous night, and the Germans had a practice of bombing the same city for several nights in succession. (This was not the massive raid which destroyed the cathedral, which had taken place a year earlier.)

Topsy, who was short, plump and jolly, took me confidently in hand. Before we boarded our double-decker, destination Walsall, she checked my skill with the punch, clipper and wallet with which I had been provided and tested me on the fares, ordinary, return and the early morning workman's fare, with which I was thoroughly muddled. Then we boarded the bus, which was already packed with passengers standing chest to chest. The journey was punishing mentally as well as physically, for one had to calculate the fares and keep records on the waybill at every stage as well as pushing through the swaying bodies and running up and down stairs, all the time keeping up a cross-talk act with the regular passengers. At this early hour, most of them were workmen going home from the night shift who knew Topsy well and made witty enquiries about her lady friend. 'Bit tall for the job, isn't she?', 'We're sorry you've got the sack', and so on. At one point the topdeckers burst into a mildly insinuating song, like extras in a scene from a Réné Clair film.

Our later journeys were more dignified, though the bus was just as full, and every time it lurched I trod on somebody's feet or fell into the lap of a passenger, squashing a shopping basket or a baby, and occasionally tempers were frayed. Our day finished at 3.30 p.m., but we had had a long break for lunch; shift times were movable and the average working week was sixty hours, which would earn a wage of from £3 15s. to £4.

My second day as a clippie was easier, for I had got my balance and learned the names of the bus-stops and the fares. On my third day I was allowed to conduct the bus for one return journey by myself. I undercharged several passengers to avoid argument and lost contact with the the waybill, but I enjoyed the humanity of the job and wondered why London clippies, unlike Topsy, were so notoriously bad-tempered.

Ventures into Welfare

Two other stories which I wrote for *Picture Post* were planned to give men in the front line a little good cheer.

A few weeks after I joined the magazine I opened a fund to provide woollies for merchant seamen. Drawing on my old knitting knowledge, now somewhat rusty, I had samples made up of sweaters, gloves and seaboot stockings in thick oiled wool, and took them to the port of Harwich to photograph them on a crew of trawlermen. I was advised that these items were desperately needed, though there was a glut of woolly helmets and scarves. I had hoped that *Picture Post* could adopt its own trawler, making the fund personal, but the authorities, who had given me the necessary passes to go on board the trawler, said that to pick one boat would be invidious and likely to cause bitterness, so the garments were to go to the comforts store on the quay at Harwich, which served the crews of both trawlers and minesweepers.

Our trawler crew played up well and we published some pictures verging on the ham of the men trying on their sweaters, gloves and stockings, together with knitting instructions and an appeal for garments, which poured in so fast that I had to wade through piles of parcels to get to my desk. My secretary and I sorted the woollies and the Hulton Press management packed them and delivered them to Harwich for as long as our readers continued to send them.

I am less sure about the wisdom of my other venture into welfare. I suggested, and Tom Hopkinson agreed, that we should give a Christmas party for some of the Americans serving in Britain – the year was 1942, the fourth Christmas of the war. I discussed it with a welfare officer in the US Air Force and he directed me to a bomber station in the Midlands where there had been heavy casualties among the Flying Fortress crews and there was an underlying gloom. I went to see the commander of the station to fix a date and other details, and then enquired in the neighbourhood for a possible venue for the party. I wanted a private house rather than a hotel, preferably a picturebook English home, and was told that a Mrs Tabor, who lived in a Tudor manor house near by, was particularly hospitable to men in the services.

I went to see her and found a saint. Yes, we could borrow the house and she would spend the night with friends. Looking round the panelled drawing-room and well-stocked library and noting the fine period furniture, I quailed, and asked her if she would like more time to think it over. 'No, I've made up my mind.' She would put away the most fragile objects and we were to clear up after the party.

There was now some hard scrounging to be done for party food and decorations. I had thought of an American menu, with fried chicken, rye whisky, Coca-Cola and ice-cream, but we couldn't get the materials. We settled for a tolerable cold buffet with American salads and pumpkin pies and an odd assortment of drinks. We booked a four-piece band from London, who gave their services for next to nothing, we were presented with a Christmas tree, and found old stocks of crackers, decorations, candles, hats and balloons.

But what about girls? A number of the *Picture Post* secretaries were crazy to go and I collected a few fashion models, adding some of my own older and steadier friends for ballast. Our management provided transport, drinks and crockery and, even more important, a posse of middle-aged men chosen for their size and weight, in case the party got rough. The US Air Force sent a stalwart sergeant in charge of the boys with the same idea.

We were under the misapprehension that the boys might be shy on arrival, perhaps detailed against their will to attend a genteel British evening, so we served each with a glass of rum punch on arrival to get the party going. It was superfluous. The party swung from the start, and for many hours American airmen and English girls sang songs, jitterbugged, danced the conga until the oak beams groaned, some of the boys gave an impromptu cabaret and we taught them the Lambeth Walk. It was not until the small hours that the sergeant called up the trucks to take his party home, having invited us to visit the airfield and look over the Flying Fortresses the next day.

I cannot remember now where my contingent was staying – perhaps the villagers helped – but in the morning the girls visited the airfield while our men heroically cleared up every crumb of food and scrap of tinsel in the manor house. When I later telephoned Mrs Tabor to thank her and to ask if anything had been damaged she said, 'One or two things will have to be repaired, but I will see to that.' As I said, a saint. I had myself put away the Hepplewhite chairs in a locked bedroom.

There was bad news from the base a few weeks later. It suffered heavy losses in a raid over Germany and several of our friends had been shot down, including the sergeant, though I believe a few were taken prisoner and long afterwards reached home. I wondered if our contribution to morale had been of any real use, for we could entertain only a tiny proportion of the hundreds of airmen at a single base. But women all over the country opened their homes to men from overseas that Christmas, some, I discovered, encouraged by our feature, so perhaps we made a few men feel a little less far from home.

OPPOSITE

Reporting for Picture Post *early in the war on community jam-making to preserve food, making a kitchen garden indoors and judging clothes for lasting value. The window-box gardener is Constance Spry.* Bottom left: *Bert Hardy, the* Picture Post *photographer with whom all the journalists liked to work.*

Later in the war, the author learned bus-conducting in Coventry, photographed government-sponsored Utility Clothes on Deborah Kerr, and organized a Christmas party for American airmen. In 1944, when she married Macdonald Hastings, Picture Post *photographer Felix H. Mann took the picture above as a wedding present.*

Some post-war snapshots.

Opposite above left: *Nannie Strafford, the benevolent autocrat who ruled the family for twenty years.*

Opposite above right: Max, *at his christening at* Aldworth Church *in* April 1946, *already knew where he was going.*

Above and opposite below: *playing with* Max *and* Clare *in a field near* Rose Cottage. Mac *took the pictures.*

Business as Usual

You and your friends born after the war often seem to be surprised that so many people lived in London and other target cities all through the war and came through unscathed. Myself for one. You know that in the winter of 1940–1 German bombs fell night after night on London, destroying entire districts, and wonder that one did not die of fright even if one was not a physical casualty. But in between the crises life was calm enough, merely uncomfortable, and when the dark, noisy nights were over, the day seemed particularly bright. According to A.J.P. Taylor (and other historians) the blitz was in fact a minor event, and the war was not seriously engaged until the Germans invaded Russia in June 1941, though it would have been galling if he had told us so at the time.

I was in London throughout the war except for occasional weekends, brief holidays and such journalistic assignments as took me into the country. Yet my personal accidents were few, and the loss of friends light in number, though they left holes in my life which never filled.

My only physical brush with the enemy was when I was bombed out of a flat in Westminster which I was sharing temporarily with Sally Chilver and her brother-in-law, and one night, after we had gone to bed, a bomb fell in the street outside. The windows crashed in, tiny fragments of shrapnel lodged in my hair – the rest of me was under the bedclothes – and I suffered small, superficial burns. The rest of the night was a misery, the three of us sitting wrapped in blankets in a corridor listening to the explosions, and longing for the all-clear siren, which usually came at dawn. I was thoroughly frightened, but we managed to chat in a desultory way. Next day, after anointing my burns, I went as usual to the office, but this was not in the least brave. I was young, youth is the secret of quick recovery from shock, and most people worked normally after much more formidable experiences.

My poor father was not so lucky. He was bombed out of our family house in Bayswater, blown out of bed by a direct hit on the house next door. Though our house fell about him, he was not apparently physically hurt, but suffered shock severe enough to bring on diabetes, which was never cured. Our shattered house had eventually to be pulled down, Daddy was given some government compensation, and it was rebuilt in a hideous modern style which is an eyesore in the pretty street.

I lost four friends in the war, three on active service, one a civilian. A close friend from my Oxford days was killed in an air crash, the young film director, Pen Tennyson, who was in the 'wavy navy', or Royal Naval Volunteer Reserve. I was sitting on a bus one day next to a man who was reading the *Evening Standard*, glanced over his shoulder and saw Pen's photograph on the front page. I grabbed the paper, read the news, but could scarcely take it in. The loss grew on me slowly over the years.

Three other close friends were killed, a young naval officer whose ship went down in the Mediterranean, my *Vogue* friend, Mollie Fordham, and, worst of all, the husband of my dearest friend from my *Vogue* days, Mary Horsman, now Mary Phipps. She had married a bomber pilot who failed to return from a raid and whose exact fate was never known. He was 'presumed killed'; no other details were given. Mary was living in Bath at the time with her young baby, my godson, and she sent me a laconic telegram at my office in *Picture Post*. I tried to telephone her but could not get through and had to content myself with the cold comfort of a telegram. I could have murdered the girl at the telephone exchange when I pleaded for a connection to be asked, 'Don't you know there's a war on?' Mollie Fordham's death was a loss to journalism as well as to her friends. She had helped to evacuate her son's school safely to an island in the Caribbean, and her ship was torpedoed on her way back to England to rejoin the fray.

These blows were spread out over several years and in between life was more normal than your generation can easily understand. There was none of the hysteria of the First World War when idiot women, unbalanced perhaps by the ghastly casualty lists, pressed white feathers on any man in a civvy suit, and when stones were thrown at dachshunds, most amiable of German beasts.

Of course everyday existence could be difficult and frustrating, not helped by the irritating slogans mouthed by well-meaning people. When you missed the last bus some bystander was sure to say, 'You'll have to take Shanks' pony', and some busybody would butt into a mildly scandalous conversation with, 'Careless talk costs lives.'

Public services were often cut off, electricity and gas being the most painful, as one was sometimes frightfully cold. The telephone was patchy, long-distance calls often taking hours. Most foods were rationed, with increasing stringency as the war went on, and some were reserved for children and hospitals, but thanks to magnificently fair distribution, nobody went hungry. Petrol rationing meant a stingy use of one's car and public transport was pretty good hell, especially on the railways, which were prime targets for enemy bombers, and a bomb fifty miles away could disrupt the whole system. More than once I slept in a station waiting-room, having missed a late-night connection. But one became street-wise. One kept some sort of camp fuel handy at home, even sticks in the fireplace, so that one could always boil a kettle. One never took a train journey without some food in one's pocket, a bun or a Spam sandwich. One cultivated the Free French, who had a club in London where the food was excellent. When the Yanks arrived *en masse*, one greeted them with unnatural ardour, for they were generous with their supplies of sweets and cigarettes from the 'PX', their servicemen's store, and would sometimes present one with an orange. On train journeys, one learned how to grab a first-class sleeper if some VIP with a reservation failed to turn up.

People varied in their attitude to taking shelter from the various forms of bombardment. As you know from Henry Moore's famous shelter drawings, the London underground stations were adapted as night shelters for those in need, and thousands of bunks were provided for those who were allotted tickets, who made a ghastly party of their nights underground, with tea parties and singsongs. Personally, if I took a tube home at night, I shuddered at these foetid gatherings and could not wait to get up to ground level and fresh air. My idea of hell would be Hitler's bunker.

In the first winter of the blitz (1940–1) most of the bombing took place by night, but later forms of attack were by day and Londoners took, or affected to take, little notice. If you were in the street when you heard a buzz-bomb, a bomb first launched in 1944 which hummed like a giant mosquito and then cut out, to be followed some seconds later by an explosion on the ground, the sensible thing might have been to throw yourself flat on the pavement when the buzzing stopped. But so great is the British fear of looking a fool that everyone just kept on walking. I once saw a man dive under the table in a restaurant when the buzzing cut out, but the poor fellow was an American who had just arrived in England, and he emerged red-faced and apologetic.

London did seem alarming when one had enjoyed an exceptional break. I once went to Scotland to spend a few days with my old knitting friend, Chris Haskett-Smith. Her husband's regiment had been posted to Inverness and Chris and Victor had quarters in a charming farmhouse on the moors where there was total peace, plentiful food including butter and cream, and enough petrol for Chris to meet me in a car. When she saw me off on the train home she pressed a basket of food and drink into my hands, much needed as the journey took nearly two days. When the train reached London at last, there was an alert on, and I felt quite nervous, for I had lost my immunity to the racket.

Looking back, though I worked extremely hard on *Picture Post*, I seem to have done very little in the way of war work. Before the war, soon after Munich, volunteers were asked to register as reserve ambulance drivers, and I had sent in my name, taken some training and passed the special driving test, but in the event only full-time, fully trained men and women were wanted in London, and I was never called on. My only contribution to defence was a weekly stint of firewatching, which meant being on call to man a stirrup-pump and learning how to crawl through a smoke-filled room, but not so much as a small incendiary bomb came my way, which tends to confirm A.J.P. Taylor's dismissive judgement on the blitz.

It must seem strange to you that the life of a civilian in the last war could be so ordinary. Surely in any future world war no living creature will be immune.

The Pursuit of Food

We spent a lot of time in the war thinking about food, and I wrote many features on the subject for *Picture Post*. Though most foods were scarce, rationing was accepted by all as fair, and the only consistently popular politician of my lifetime was the wartime Minister of Food, Lord Woolton. He was a brilliant administrator and a mass psychologist, too.

Our preoccupation with food was really a sort of hobby. Though we were not hungry, for the allowed rations were adequate and obtainable, much ingenuity went into providing 'extras', particularly in the country, where there was scope for reviving ancient peasant culinary lore. Some of these food economies sound a bit cranky today, but others survived into times of plenty. As you know, I still make nettle soup.

I have told you that I collaborated quite often with Constance Spry, who was then living in an old farmhouse with a large garden in Kent. Constance, a marvellous woman made up of energy and idealism in equal measure, made her reputation in the thirties as a flower arranger, but she was just as talented as a gardener and a cook. Her crusade from the early days of the war was to promote gardening for the pot, and her policy was to grow only quality vegetables and to cook them for the main course, not as a side dish – she despised 'meat and two veg'. She said that it was as easy to grow a choice vegetable as a coarse one, and she gave me main course recipes for *Petits Pois à la Française*, using 'a good, small, round-seeded pea', for calabrese (then very little grown in England) served in bundles like asparagus, and for sweet corn served in browned margarine. Sweet corn, again, was not much grown in Britain before the war, as we mistakenly considered our climate too cold. For women living in towns she urged pots of herbs and tomatoes on the balcony or window-sill and sea-kale in the cellar.

A few weeks later I was off to interview a businessman in Hertfordshire who was turning his garden into an amateur smallholding – he had an enthusiasm for geese, probably misplaced – and later again I discovered a country housewife who was an expert at cooking with wild weeds. Dandelion and wood sorrel salad, elderflower fritters, purée of Good King Henry, rose-hip jam, herb sandwich-spread and stinging nettles on toast were among the recipes which I gaily offered our readers in a leaflet. With hindsight, I doubt if all these recipes were practical, as leaves of wild plants shrink sadly in the cooking and it would be difficult to gather enough to make a substantial meal. True, poor country people have used wild plants for food extensively throughout history, but often they were hungry to starvation point, and the whole family would go picking to keep alive.

Some wartime cooking was a communal effort, especially in the case of food preserving. When there was a glut of fruit or vegetables, with lean times ahead, many villages would devote a day or more to making jam or canning produce at a Fruit Preservation Centre, probably organized by the Women's Institute, and canning machines were passed from village to village. Individual efforts at preservation went beyond conventional jam making and fruit bottling, and all of us who had access to the country dried apple rings and mushrooms, salted runner beans in crocks, pickled onion thinnings, and dried peas and herbs. 'I can let you have reliable recipes for all types of preserving,' I wrote confidently in *Picture Post*. I think the recipes must have been sound enough, for I continued to dry apple rings and thread mushrooms on strings long after the war, or until the deep-freeze made drying and canning obsolete. Other communal ventures were concerned with marketing surplus produce, and a country friend of mine collected a carload of vegetables from the community once a week and sold them to the Women's Institute stall in the nearest town, so that food was rescued which would have been wasted.

Vegetable gardening, a long neglected skill, was reborn in the war and 'Dig for Victory' was a slogan so overworked that we grew sick to death of it. Most gardeners continued to grow a few flowers, but scrapped the lawn and planted it with vegetables, and gardeners became thrifty, saving seed and storing root vegetables in clamps.

As the war progressed, the food we ate became increasingly eccentric. Dehydrated foods to save shipping space came in in 1942. Four ounces of dried egg powder were the equivalent of nine large fresh eggs and two ounces of dried potato equalled fourteen ounces of fresh potato. Not very tasty, either of them, but we ate them, along with such innovations as whalemeat, rook pie and Spam. Good cooks did ingenious things with dried eggs, such as scrambling them with curry powder, and dried cabbage could be made into a purée once you had reinflated it, so to speak. The Ministry of Food issued regular leaflets which caused much merriment. War Cookery Leaflet no.11 included recipes for English Monkey (a mess of dried eggs) and Mock Fried Egg, which began, 'Cut holes from the centre of each slice of bread with a stone cutter and pour half an egg into each hole.'

We talked and thought frequently about food, but it was a harmless preoccupation, much less self-indulgent than today's obsession with health, and many of us learned to cook who didn't know the rudiments before. In fact, I doubt if you *can* cook until you have made an omelette with margarine, dried egg and chopped chickweed. Where did the great Reform Club chef, Alexis Soyer, meet and overcome his strongest challenge? With the troops in the Crimean War.

When eating away from home one fared better or worse according to the skill of the establishment or the depth of its involvement in the black market. Good eating places were likely to be London clubs, remote country hotels and farmhouses, where shortages were few owing to the barter system. 'Where there's mutton there's tea', a hospitable sheep farmer in Cumberland explained to me. Private entertaining depended on the character of the host or hostess. It was supposed to be the decent thing, if entertaining, to stint oneself for a few days and keep the meat ration for the guests, but this was not always the custom. It is illuminating to read the wartime diaries of social characters whose work kept them constantly on the move.

James Lees-Milne's *Ancestral Voices*, which has much in common with Surtees' *Mr Sponge's Sporting Tour*, comments cuttingly on some of the many hosts who entertained him while he was travelling through England for the National Trust. 'I had a horrible day with Colonel Pemberton at Pyrland Hall near Taunton,' he wrote in 1943. 'He gave me an exiguous lunch of bread and cheese, both hard as wood, a baked potato in its skin, dry as sawdust, and watery apple pie with Bird's custard. Ugh!' One is irresistibly reminded of Jawleyford Court towards the end of Mr Sponge's visit, when he was put on short commons to drive him away. Nor did the Berkeley Hotel treat Lees-Milne much better. 'Luncheon cost 17*s*. for two, without drinks. It consisted of indifferent thick soup made of God knows what, minced chicken hash and no pudding. Really scandalous.' He found the meals less frugal wherever there was game, which was unrationed. At Rudyard Kipling's old home, Bateman's, he got 'a delicious dinner of partridge and Château Haut-Brion claret, 1920', and at Stourhead 'we had soup, whiting, pheasant, apple pie, dessert, a white Rhine wine and port'.

I mustn't give the impression that Jim Lees-Milne's diaries are chiefly about food. Their main subject is country house architecture, upon which he is always illuminating. But they do confirm that we gave much thought to food in every walk of life, licking our lips over those tempting 'extras'.

Rosamond Lehmann

For a period of two or three years in the war Rosamond Lehmann came to live in Aldworth, as surreal a vision in our quiet village as a magnolia in a cornfield. Indeed her residence at Diamond Cottage, which shared a boundary with Rose Cottage, was itself a freak situation created by the exigencies of the war. Rosamond loved the country as a source of aesthetic experience and appreciated every wisp of pink cloud made rosy by the sunset and every diamond icicle frozen by frost on thaw. But she had lived formerly in manor houses with gardeners and cooks to protect her from the harsher realities of village life and had no more idea of how to sow broad beans or pluck a pheasant than I had of how to write a tragic novel. Throughout her stay in Aldworth she was blessed with a living-in cook-housekeeper past call-up age so that she could rise above the meaner chores and carry on her proper business in life, which was writing very, very good novels. She had a son and a daughter at boarding school who came to Aldworth for the holidays. Visitors were frequent, mostly poets.

Rosamond was arrestingly and exotically beautiful, a precious orchid of a woman, part Jewish, with all the cleverness and sensibilities of her race. Tall and Junoesque, she was haloed in curls of blue-rinsed hair (it had gone white when she was in her twenties) framing a serious face with enormous eyes, full lips and the most perfect skin I have ever seen. She dressed strikingly, often in cherry-red trousers with an angora sweater outlining her ripe figure. Her voice was soft, her *bons-mots*, not always free from malice, uttered almost in gasps.

The difficulty about Rosamond as a neighbour was that she was so exquisitely sensitive that she made everyone else feel plain thick. Though she and I were much of a height she was certainly two stone heavier, yet I felt lumbering in her presence, clumsy of movement, coarse in perception, deaf to fine feelings and hard of voice. As for for your father, she frankly dismissed him as an oaf. Her book of short stories called *The Gypsy's Baby* contained one story about our village, the characters thinly disguised, and at first I wondered if I was the 'filthy-tempered woman' who quarrelled with the vicar or one of the bogus journalists who were, according to the vicar, 'not respectable, got up like street-walkers'; but on enquiry I discovered that the filthy-tempered woman was another neighbour, who rode to hounds and was familiar with the language of the hunting field, and I did not see how I could be the tarty journalist as I dressed very simply and was at least as respectable as Rosamond, who had a celebrated lover, the poet Cecil Day-Lewis. Perhaps I was the 'harum-scarum lady' who was always tearing about on a bicycle. The heroine of Rosamond's story was a woman of unblemished perfection who lived for others, sympathizing with their troubles and cooking their chops. She had a boy and a girl at boarding-school, just like Rosamond herself, who perhaps saw herself as a Mrs Miniver.

She did not have much in the way of a cottager's instincts. I remember her once picking mushrooms with Cecil, who always wore a dark city overcoat in the country and carried an umbrella. She often reproached me for getting up earlier than she did and getting the best of the crop. 'Are you taking them to market?' she once asked me drily, eyeing my brimming basket, and I admit that I had picked rather a lot, but I used to dry them for the winter.

Rosamond could just tolerate me, as I had literary forebears – she knew and rather liked my father, loathed my mother – but your father and Rosamond ground against each other like pieces of broken machinery. Early in their acquaintance they were chatting over the boundary hedge when Rosamond apologized for the forlorn state of her garden, which was indeed terrible, the village gardeners having been called up and Rosamond not handy with a spade. 'Yes, it is pretty awful', said your father, disdaining tact and not offering to help her. 'You'll have to dig it all up and weed it from end to end.' On another occasion, when she had guests to stay, she invited us to Sunday lunch. One of her guests was the poet Laurie Lee, and we found him wandering on Sunday morning in our garden gathering a bunch of snowdrops. Your father was annoyed that he had not asked our permission, but took a terrible revenge over lunch.

We had an excellent meal of roast leg of lamb, which was truly generous of Rosamond, as good meat was on coupons and supplies were tight. When we had cleared our plates Rosamond asked, 'Will anyone have some more of these lovely vegetables?' and your father said, 'Yes, please, and I'll have some more meat, too.' I blushed for him and made him give her the last pheasant of the season the following weekend.

Your father excepted, every man in the village and beyond was slightly in love with Rosamond, such was her fascination. She was a true *femme fatale*. The grumpy officer in the Home Guard who had a plan to put a machine-gun nest in my bedroom (an aged survivor of the first war who could have been a model for Dad's Army) hung on her words, as did the retired bank manager in the large modern house on the downs whose wife had fled to America leaving him a prey to thoughts of romance. The baker adored her, too and, just a little bit, the vicar. Your father alone seemed to be immune.

In due course, Rosamond sold the modest cottage and moved to London. The village seemed dull without her imperiousness and her beauty, and she was much missed. Later, when life struck her two cruel blows, the defection of her lover and the untimely death of her beloved daughter, she retreated more and more into the private world of her intense emotions and I came to realize that she was not only a beautiful writer but a very strong woman.

Bert Hardy

Of all the photographers I worked with on *Picture Post* the most companionable was Bert Hardy. Some of our assignments were far away in the provinces, and the travelling conditions might be rugged, with crowded or even benighted trains, scarce food and sordid hotels, but Bert always made the trip more of an adventure than a slog.

Bert was (still is, I'm glad to say) the quintessential cockney, with the ready wit and powers of improvisation of Sam Weller. The eldest of seven children, he was born in south London near the Elephant and Castle, left school at fourteen and started work as a messenger in a photographic business at ten shillings a week. From this meagre wage he contrived to save up for a camera, learned to take pictures and quickly acquired an assured technique – the eye for a picture was inborn. He viewed his fellow man with affection and humour and almost unconsciously caught the irony of a situation or the character behind a face. He saw the rueful twist in the cheery smile of a soldier on his way to war, the pomposity behind the smoothness of some great man of affairs, the anxious longing of a girl in love. Added to his penetrating eye and sleight of hand with a camera was a high personal courage, and the male journalists who went with him on the rougher assignments, perhaps in the blitz, on a convoy at sea, or in battle, said that when he picked up the camera slung round his neck, all danger was forgotten.

He usually carried one camera only, occasionally two, either a Leica or a Contax, and he did not take an enormous number of photographs, preferring to select his shots with care. 'Remember', he told me later, 'that in those days you had to wind on each exposure by hand and you might be working at a terrific pace. You couldn't waste time taking dud shots.' Among his most famous stories were a feature on that grim district of the Glasgow slums, the Gorbals, a feature on life at the Elephant and Castle, and, after the world war, a reportage on the Korean war in 1950, with James Cameron as the journalist. This was sadly the cause of the sacking of Tom Hopkinson as editor of *Picture Post* by the proprietor, Edward Hulton, Hulton banning its publication for political reasons, and Tom refusing to accept the censorship. Eventually the pictures were published all over the world and won the *Encyclopaedia Britannica* World Prize of the Year.

Bert had not an aitch to his name, nor a 'th' either. We were once at Paddington Station buying tickets to Theale in Berkshire. 'Two tickets to Fill,' he said to the booking clerk. 'To where?' 'To Fill, I told you.' 'Never heard of it.' 'Bert, you're not trying, you can say Theale if you want to.' 'Fill.' As a hostile queue was drawing up behind us, I asked for the tickets in my ladylike voice.

Travelling with Bert was an education in the art of survival. Nobody could call him good-looking. He had a bulbous nose in a purplish face, but his charm moved mountains. We were once on a horrible journey to Liverpool which seemed eternal, the train crawling because there had been bombs somewhere up the line, when we stopped at a station where there was a buffet, which seemed to be open. The passengers poured out and swarmed for the buffet only to find that there was no tea or food left, not so much as a Spam sandwich. The whistle blew, the disappointed passengers poured back, with Bert last of all carrying two steaming cups of tea. 'How on earth did you manage it?' I asked. 'I just patted the girl's hand, like, and it turned out she had a spoonful of tea left, so she made it fresh.' We were not popular in the carriage.

Bert was always a gifted acquirer of rationed food and scarce commodities. He had only to look at a lorry for a crate to fall off the back of it. He was generous with this loot in the office and sweets, tea, cigarettes and even gin would appear with remarkable frequency, Bert charging different rates to friends and foes. 'Oh, Bert, I can't,' I once said priggishly when he offered me a box of chocolates. 'You can't have seen yet another overloaded lorry.' 'Anne, I promise you, I ran and ran after that lorry when I saw the crate fall off, but I couldn't catch it up.' I buried my scruples.

On his travels, Bert left many bruised hearts behind, so great was his skill in the art of chatting up girls. He was a genuine romantic and sometimes, when he had waved goodbye to a pretty girl whom he had engaged in a mild flirtation, he would sit quiet and thoughtful in the train going home. Though intensely proud of his cockney background, he appreciated the comforts of a more sophisticated life. Once, staying in a better hotel than the usual wartime dump, our breakfast toast was brought in in toastracks, which greatly impressed him. After breakfast he bought a toastrack as a present for his wife, saying he looked forward to having his toast cut into triangles at home. '*And I mean to have the crusts cut off.*'

In 1990, I wanted to talk to Bert about the old days and asked him to lunch with me in a Soho restaurant to find that he had not changed in a single respect, even in appearance. He ordered stewed eels, still his favourite dish, which he washed down with red wine and whisky. I said, 'Lunch is on you next time, Bert', when it turned out in the course of conversation that he was richer than I am. He had been as lucky with property as he had been with rationed food, and still owns a small, valuable house near the Elephant and Castle as well as a farm in Surrey. After *Picture Post* folded in 1957, Bert worked in advertising with immense rewards, both financial and prestigious; he superintended many exhibitions of his work and published a successful autobiography.

'Can you say Theale?' I asked when he had finished his stewed eels and I my scallops on a skewer. 'Fill', he answered.

Marriage

Our marriage started bumpily, with your father's dash to Normandy to catch up with the Second Front. Mac was a lion of a journalist, always on the scene of action, and when I first met him he was on crutches. He had been in a car smash and was in hospital when I joined the staff, and returned to the office looking pale but resolute.

When I arrived at *Picture Post* they ran a feature in the paper introducing me, with appropriately glamorous photographs, and Mac told everybody but me that he had seen the pictures in his hospital bed and said, 'I'm going to marry that girl.'

Writing in later years about his wartime team Tom Hopkinson tended to write down Mac Hastings as an expert on country matters, a subject which was in fact his second string. In the war years he rushed gallantly into every fray, reporting from battleships, bombers and, now, the Second Front. Soon after the war, when the urbane clergyman from Lancashire, the Revd Marcus Morris, launched *Eagle* magazine for boys for Hulton Press, Mac became its staff Action Man, personally sampling such daredevil activities as parachute jumping, steeplejacking, and riding the Cresta Run. Though physically wiry, he wasn't a natural athlete, so that his exploits demanded a rare screwing up of courage.

In the war, the niceties of personal relationships were often swamped by the universal struggle for national survival. One was simply too busy to ask oneself, 'What will he or she be like when the excitement is over and one will be sharing one's time and thoughts quietly with another human being?' Mac and I admired each other and enjoyed the limited time we spent in each other's company. We lived together for a time in my Chelsea flat, from which Lesley Blanch had moved, and then we got married, your father proposing to me in fishing terms – 'I mean to hook you' – so I ought to have known it was a mistake. As you know, we were eventually divorced, but not for eighteen years, and though I knew much happiness in my children, my marriage lacked any depth of feeling on my side, and I think on your father's too. He used to say cheerily, 'I've got the three things I wanted most, a Churchill gun, a Hardy rod, and a beautiful wife,' and he wasn't being funny. I strongly resented being counted as a chattel with a gun and a rod, and retreated more and more into my private thoughts.

I blame nobody for the break-up. The truth is that we were two decent people who deceived ourselves in the heat of war into believing that we had common tastes, but were totally incompatible. Mac was very right-wing, I am a convinced liberal. He liked sporting people, I liked artists. His ideal holiday was deer-stalking in Scotland, mine was church-crawling in France. He had a passion for firearms, which terrify me. We both liked the country, but Mac saw it as a theatre for field sports and I liked looking for flowers in the fields. Relations grew really bitter at the time of Suez, when I lost my cool for once and we had a row which smouldered for days. Mac saw the Suez venture as a blow struck for England, and Anthony Eden as a hero, and I thought it an act of barbarism. Our attitudes were poles apart.

Though we never shared a close relationship we were usually friendly enough on the surface and rubbed along reasonably well for a good many years. Twice in the course of our marriage I experienced overwhelming joy, when Max was born on 28 December 1945 and again when you were born on 2 October 1951, and from the day of Max's arrival, when we became a small family, not just an ill-assorted couple, my loneliness eased.

After the war Mac left *Picture Post* to become editor of the *Strand Magazine*, which he fought valiantly to bring back to life. He made it particularly strong on illustration, and Ardizzone, Osbert Lancaster, Louis de Brocquy and others of that calibre regularly illustrated its pages. But the monthly general-interest magazines were by then a doomed institution; the *Strand* lost money and was closed in 1950. Mac was deeply upset. However, he was already writing successful thrillers, and made a new career in television, joining the famous BBC *Tonight* team, where he specialized in features on animals. I remember watching him on the screen handling a particularly tricky ferret, and on another occasion demonstrating the art of training gun dogs. Recalling the fate of some of our own domestic pets (watch this space), I think that his affection for animals was deeper than his practical knowledge thereof.

Rose Cottage continued to be, if not a bond between us, at least a cheerfully shared habitation, and we went there every weekend with Max, Nannie* and, later, with you, too. We both enjoyed not only the cottage but the whole village of Aldworth, which, as you know, has a feudal system of its own. The old manor house, De la Bèche, was rebuilt long ago, there is no hereditary lord of the manor, and the cottages in the village are are either council-owned or freeholds, but all of us are vassals of the McQuhae family, who have run the Bell Inn for five generations, at first as tenants, now as owner-landlords. You won't remember the Mr McQuhae of my early days in the village, a dour Scot so grumpy to customers that the pub was always empty, but his genial daughter Heather rules us all, a pillar of the parish, and is the moving spirit in fund-raising, geese-rearing, pig-roasting, daffodil-growing, cricket-management and the planning of extraordinary outings, such as the village day trip on Concorde which (regrettably to us seeking after peace and quiet) drew a BBC filming crew and put the pub all too clearly on the map. Under the benevolent rule of Heather and her handsome husband, Ian Macaulay, the Bell is not only a pub but the village club, and it is quite possible to be blackballed. The village shop and post office, too, are in McQuhae hands, run by Heather's sister, Maureen, another pillar of parish and church.

On those long-ago weekends at the cottage, your father spent his time shooting or fishing and then took up riding, so I did not see much of him. I devoted every possible hour to making the garden, shaping the steep, awkward site, planting fruit-trees and shrubs for the future and bulbs and border plants for quicker delight. If our marriage was inwardly barren, it was rarely acrimonious.

*I inherited Nanny Strafford, a doughty Yorkshire woman, from Mary Phipps a few weeks after Max was born. Of her benevolent tyranny, more anon.

The Smallholders

I am not sure when your father decided that he was a born smallholder, but I think it was early in 1945, when the war was clearly drawing to a close. Already we had more time to get to the country than in the critical years and, a key factor, the cottager next door to Rose Cottage, Mr Dobson, who had helped with my garden before he was called up, was released from his wartime job in an ordnance factory. Dobson was an inarticulate son of the soil straight out of *Cold Comfort Farm*, but he had a good understanding of domestic animals. Though optimism was not in his nature, he seemed willing to help us look after a chicken or two, or even something more ambitious.

A few years earlier, in 1941, when many civilians were digging for victory or keeping backyard hens, I had interviewed an amateur smallholder for *Picture Post* and I now turned up the files and studied his advice.

'Don't rush out and buy a few animals at random,' he had said. 'Stock-keeping is difficult today. All foodstuffs are scarce, and most of them are rationed. Before you buy a single chick you must ask yourself, "Can I feed it? Can I collect scraps for it? Can I grow special food for it?" You should lay your plans weeks or months before you buy your stock.' But your father would have none of this slow and steady approach, and plunged in recklessly.

'Ark coops are the thing for chickens', he told me with his usual buoyant confidence. 'You put the coop on the lawn and move it on every day, so there is no mucking out and the chickens always have a fresh supply of grass. The chicken manure will also stimulate the growth of new grass, so we might manage a few geese. We'll look after the chickens at the weekend and Dobson will cope in the week, and we'll share the eggs.'

'But what will we feed them on?' I asked. 'We won't qualify for a cereal ration, we've no kale, and I can't sow sunflowers until the soil warms up.'

'Oh, we'll get some corn somewhere and feed them up on hot mashes. You must keep a pot on the go for vegetable peelings and collect kitchen scraps, and we'll glean sacks of corn in harvest time.'

Within days – not the weeks or months that the smallholder had recommended – your father had bought a mobile ark coop. Then he bought six Black Leghorn hens in full lay. He scrounged a little corn, I started the hot mashes, which smelt disgusting, and the hens laid about twenty eggs in the first week. I felt like Little Red Riding Hood I collected them in my wicker basket. In the second week the output dropped to twelve eggs, and in the fourth week there was one. Clearly the hot mashes were not sufficiently nourishing.

By May 1945 I knew that I was pregnant and your father thought, more by association of ideas than a process of reasoning, that what we needed was a cow. I declined to keep a cow on our own premises, but Dobson was willing to house it in his shed. Your father bought a lovely small Guernsey cow called Carmen. I bought milk pans, a skimmer, various jugs and a small churn.

I truly loved Carmen, a compliant and affectionate creature with huge beautiful eyes which I remember as azure blue, though this may be a romantic fiction. Carmen's milk was for quite a long time plentiful and extremely rich. Dobson milked her and Mrs Dobson and I shared the tasks of skimming and churning and we had a good supply of cream and butter. When in due course Carmen ran dry, we asked a farmer for advice as to what to do next, and he examined Carmen, said she was a very old cow, probably incapable of bearing another calf, and we must send her to market. This we did, but I was very upset, though your father said that farming was no place for sentimentality.

Our final experiment was more successful. Your father bought a pig and Dobson built a pigsty. I don't remember a thing about the pig, not even its name, except that it seemed quite satisfied with the food provided and grew really fat. In due course it went to be killed and we had the hams cured and, though rather too salt, they were an asset to the larder and a talking point at masculine gatherings, your father chiding any friend who did not keep a pig, even if he lived in a London flat. 'Pure profit, old boy, no expense, no trouble, and sizzling bacon at the end of the day.'

The pig was the last of our farm animals but not of our animal problems, for we had a series of 'gun dogs' at a period when your father had the lease of some rough shooting on the downs. I write the words in quotation marks for they were outrageously disobedient to your father's commands and were roundly cursed by the other guns as they started up every hare or partridge within miles. The most notorious was Ruins, a lovable but free-ranging spaniel which cut a swathe through many a shoot. Then there was the retriever Kim – well, I won't go into Kim's career. Later there was poor, dear Friday, whom of course you remember, who had spent a month with your father on his desert island adventure in the Indian Ocean, and developed a human fixation. He adored the human race and even had a human expression on his face, but detested other dogs and would fall on them savagely, so that it was a terror to take him for a walk. After one dreadful incident in which Friday murdered a sheep, I urged sending him to a dog handler to see if he could be trained, but, weeping, your father took him to the vet and had him put down.

Years later, when I was married to Osbert, there was Maud, the dachshund puppy which you and he conspired to give me for Christmas, and I shall never forget the moment of drama when you led little Maud in on Christmas morning to make her first puddle on the living-room floor. It was a total (and not wholly welcome) surprise, for you had concealed her well. 'Poor little Maud, she won't last long', I said to myself, for I was ignorant of pet care and anxious about her welfare. But Maud lived for seventeen-and-a-half years, loving me blindly to the last. She was a well-bred dog, picky with her food, and for years, on the instructions of a fashionable London vet, I cooked her delicate meals of rice with fresh chicken or rabbit and a garnish of crushed biscuit to discover, when she was twelve years old, that what she really liked was half a tin of Chum.

I don't know how to sum up my attitude to animals. I want to do my best for them and am gratified if they like me, but on the whole I am uneasy with them. The truth is that, though I love the country, and am good with plants, I was brought up a London child.

Post-war Doldrums

The years immediately after the war brought me great inner happiness with the birth of a son, but my outer life was bleak. My career entered a waste patch and the nation itself was in a sullen frame of mind.

If I believed in anything so dogmatic as a rule of life, mine would be 'never go back on your tracks', but I did this foolish thing in April 1945 when I was offered, and accepted, the editorship of *Harper's Bazaar* (now *Harper's & Queen*), which had been ticking over without an editor for several years.

Harper's Bazaar was a similar magazine to *Vogue*, devoted to fashion, beauty, interior decoration and the social world, and, though I was now the editor, not just a member of the staff, I had a disagreeable feeling of *déja vu*. After the wide-ranging experiences of *Picture Post*, I was back among the couture, the 'wholesale', the prissy photographers, the advertisers (whom I never met on *Picture Post*) demanding puffs, the temperamental model girls and the beauties of the day who wanted to be photographed one minute and changed their minds the next. (Never, ever, has any woman caused me so much trouble as Vivien Leigh.) In short, I had made a mistake.

At that time – I believe it is quite different today – *Harper's Bazaar* suffered from several disadvantages compared with *Vogue*, notably a much smaller budget, and I could offer only exiguous fees to photographers and contributors and small salaries to my staff. But I found the period itself unsympathetic to a glossy career. Clothes were rationed and were to remain so for several years to come, and the best were reserved for export. The fashion trade was crippled by shortages of fabric, accessories (there was a fearful dearth of shoes), trained work people and, above all, of talent. For six years potential designers had been employed in civilian war jobs or the forces, the young men who might have been fashion photographers had been army cameramen, the girls skilled with sewing-machines had been making parachutes, not dresses. Paper was so strictly rationed that there was no opportunity for a magazine to expand. You had your quota of paper and no more, and so great was the demand for anything to read that every publication, good, bad or indifferent, could sell every copy it could print. Books were similarly handicapped, and most books of the period were abominably produced on horrid paper, yet sold out regardless of merit. There was no competition to make a job interesting.

It was not only my personal career which slid backwards after the war. The standard of living and the morale of the whole country seemed to go downhill. Wars, accidents and natural disasters create a team spirit among the sufferers while the crisis lasts. Friendship and altruism abound. But when the danger is over, the recriminations begin, and so it was this time. In the war, if we talked to strangers in a bus or a queue it was to share large common emotions such as heartache at the sinking of a warship, but now it was to groan about the shortage of bananas. We had expected a bonanza but were plunged in material misery, for the war had made us a poor country.

I think that 1947 was the year when national grumbling reached its peak. Food was extremely short for a long time after the war, and in 1947 most staple foods were still rationed, and in some cases we were getting *less* than in 1945. This was true of bread, flour, fats, meat, bacon and ham, and also soap. We got only one egg each a week. In the spring of 1947, when a fuel crisis hit the factories, the sweet ration was cut in half. Even as late as 1950, five years after VE-day, good food was such a rare treat that Elizabeth David, writing on cookery for me at *Harper's Bazaar*, wrote an article called 'Windfalls', in which she suggested a reckless use of anything so rare and precious as a present of eggs or butter from the country. She advised us to blow 'all the available meat ration on the very best fillet steak and to make a Béarnaise sauce to go with it'.

Worst of all was the desperate shortage of fuel. The winter of 1947 was a bitter one – snow started falling in December 1946, and continued for three months, so that impassable snow drifts piled up in many parts of the country. Transport was at a standstill, coal stocks were exhausted and electricity was cut off for hours every day.

One particular source of irritation was that many other countries, even defeated ones, seemed to be better off than ourselves. We heard (probably spurious) tales of high living in Germany. We felt it ironic that Paris, which had been occupied by the Germans, should be in a position and mood to launch Dior's New Look, the most extravagant fashion, rich in colour, material and embroidery, since the heyday of King Edward VII. English dress manufacturers struggled bravely to interpret it but, hampered by austerity regulations and poor resources, their copies were inevitably feeble.

You may suggest that my reactions to this dreary period were partly subjective, but I have some evidence to the contrary. I was still writing occasional articles for *Picture Post,* and in 1947 Tom Hopkinson asked me to write a piece called 'As the Woman in the Home Sees the Crisis'. I wrote an article summing up her frustrations, as I saw them, stressing her feeling of being let down after her heroic efforts in the war – her sheer disappointment. Tom told me that it was one of the most successful articles he had ever published, for readers identified with my 'woman in the home'.

If the world around me was resentful, and my job frustrating, I had one resounding joy to compensate me. Max was born in December 1945. I cannot claim that my pregnancy was good timing, but I had been hoping for a baby for eighteen months without reward. When I found I was pregnant, almost immediately after joining *Harper's,* I went to the management and suggested retiring, but as I had started, they preferred me to carry on. In those days maternity did not go well with a job. There was no such thing as maternity leave, one was always hungry (I craved meat), and maternity and baby clothes were expensive, scarce and tightly rationed. I still remember being obliged to wear my red fitted coat for months after the buttons had ceased to fasten, an incongruous sight at a Mayfair fashion show. I promised myself that if I had another baby I would leave my job, which I did, nearly six years later. Meanwhile I did my best at *Harper's*, and I think I improved the magazine and relished every small advance. Finding British fashion in a starved state, I decided to build up the general features and I and my Features Editor, Jane Stockwood, gathered new contributors with considerable success. I was proud to publish Elizabeth David, John Betjeman, Lesley Blanch, Eric Ambler, John Mortimer and other first-rate writers, some established, some young and new.

I would call my stint at *Harper's Bazaar* a period of marking time, and six years is too long for that uncreative activity. But there were better times to come.

Firstborn

Your brother Max was an impetuous character even at the foetus stage. He was due to be born in mid-January, 1946, and my gynaecologist thought it would be quite safe for me to go off to the country for Christmas. But some instinct warned me to stay in London, which was fortunate, for had we gone away Max might well have been born somewhere between Maidenhead and Slough on the Great West Road. Always in a rush, he arrived two weeks early.

He was not the usual wrinkly baby, but a completely finished product with a purposeful expression on his face, and the midwife was convinced I had miscalculated and that, far from being early, he was two or three weeks late. He looked quite at home in the world, firmly demanded what he wanted, but never grizzled or cried for nothing. A few days after his birth, the ward sister herself handed him to me for feeding and said, smiling, 'I must warn you that this little boy is going to get very bad school reports.' A prophetess.

Thereafter, he was always 'forward'. At eighteen months, sitting up in his high chair at a seaside hotel, an admiring elderly lady said to me, 'He does enjoy his food, doesn't he?' There was no chucking his egg around or leaving his pudding unfinished. At two he spoke so fluently that he could have made a political speech. At five, when your father and I took him for an interview at Wagner's, his pre-prep school, the headmaster's wife said, not wholly with admiration, 'I have never seen such a self-possessed child.' I am sorry to say that as our party left the study for the schoolroom he had pushed her aside and gone through the door first.

Like his father, he has always enjoyed a physical challenge. At ten, he came with me to Austria in the skiing season (I was writing a story for the *Sunday Express*) and after one hour on the nursery slopes, skied back solo through the streets to our hotel. At fifteen, watching a western on television, he got so excited that he whipped a revolver from his pocket and shot the set to smithereens. At seventeen he made his first parachute jump. At twenty-two he was covering riots in America for an English newspaper, and before he was forty had been a brilliant war correspondent in the Middle East, Vietnam, Angola, India, Cyprus, Northern Ireland and the Falklands. He has written eleven books about war. His recreations are shooting and fishing.

I have always been slightly afraid of Max, whose audacious nature overpowers my cautious one, and afraid *for* Max, following his exploits from afar with my heart in my mouth. Now that he is Editor-in-Chief of the *Daily Telegraph* newspapers, with an enormous sphere of influence, I can reasonably hope that his wilder adventures are behind him. But as beyond every mountain there always seems to be another peak, I cannot be sure.

The Cult of Frinton-on-Sea

'Oh dear, the room won't do at all, Mrs Hastings, it's much too light, no proper curtains, what with all this sun pouring in I'll never get Max to sleep. Did you tell them there was a child coming?'

We had arrived, Max, Nannie and I (this was before your time – I was still editing *Harper's*) at a ravishingly pretty village in Brittany, where our hotel, whitewashed and slate-roofed, was smothered in pink climbing geraniums, and we were right on the sea. But Nannie, who had a blind spot for the picturesque, didn't care for it. The food was a poem, with fresh-caught fish and lobsters, crêpes and meringues, but Nannie said gloomily that she would pay anything for a plate of mince with fingers of toast. 'And isn't it funny, madam, the French don't seem to do much in the way of tea, not that I mind for myself, of course, but Max does enjoy his tea.' It was a difficult fortnight.

'I wonder why the service is so slow? The food is almost cold when we get it, our table being in the far corner. And we are such a long way from the beach my poor feet are tired out, and I'm sure I'm a good walker. The sands are good, I grant you, when we get there, but no shelter, I don't know what we would do in a storm.'

It was Nannie, Max and I again, this time in a family hotel in Devonshire, converted from an old farmhouse set among trees and blue hydrangeas, with a five-minute walk across fields to the sea. There was well-cooked country food, lots of children, games and entertainments, Devonshire teas daily and mince every Wednesday. But Nannie didn't care for the place. Another difficult fortnight.

'Oh, it's ever so dangerous, such a steep path down to the beach, anyone could slip, and such treacherous rocks. I couldn't let poor little Clare paddle this morning, it was so rough she would have been washed away.'

It was Cornwall, this time, at a hotel on the kind of rugged headland which had delighted my father long ago, overlooking a sandy cove with marine life for Max and sandy pools for you, who were now on the strength. Even better, your father had consented to join us for a few days and took Max sea-fishing, so I had some company. But Nannie didn't care for it.

The following year I said, 'Nannie, this year you must choose our summer holiday. Where would you like to go?'

Nannie beamed. 'Well, madam, all the nannies say it's ever so nice at Frinton, it's really select, and oh, so safe for children. When you book the rooms, be sure to book a beach-hut as well, in a central position, we don't want to be stuck at the far end of the beach.' Nannie had done her homework.

As I expect you remember, our household revolved round Nannie, who was the embodiment of nursery prejudice, and I ought to have realized sooner that she would never be happy until she had spent a holiday at the nannies' cult-place, Frinton-on-Sea. In the fifties and sixties there were still plenty of middle-aged old-fashioned nannies ruling the families they worked for, and in August they swooped on Frinton in a cloud of grey gaberdine with their little charges in tow. A number of mothers came, too, but fathers were a rare sight on the beach (some came with their families but spent the days on the golf course), and those few looked dispirited as they tried to get up a game of rounders or cricket.

Frinton was an old-fashioned nanny's idea of heaven because it involved absolutely no risk. The town was exquisitely clean, the public greensward closely mown, the gabled or turreted red-brick villas had well-kept gardens, firm, pram-worthy paths sloped gently down to the iron-grey sea. The beach was an endless stretch of unbroken sand, without a rock, cave, pool, pebble or shell to break its smooth surface or present hazards to precious little lives. As for limpets or starfish, you might as well look for a Rottweiler.

Fringing the top of the beach was a row of beach-huts, or chalets, rented by the week, and the size and position of the hut determined a nanny's status. I do not myself care for beach-huts, which always smell of decaying seaweed, but to a nanny a hut represented a small home of her own where she could dispense tea or coffee and cakes, store beachballs, towels and buckets, boil eggs on a camp cooker and make toast. Time being short, the nannies made up their holiday cliques quickly and by the second day the deckchairs had formed into regular groups where congenial friends sat talking or knitting, quite relaxed about their charges, for it would be difficult to drown at Frinton. You, dear Clare, were still young enough to be content for hours making pies and sandcastles, but Max was restless and at seven was much too old for the place. There was absolutely nothing for an active boy to do.

If Frinton was heaven for nannies, it was purgatory for me. The mornings on the beach induced an *ennui* so mind-destroying that I could not even read a book. I had an idea that we might go for some afternoon drives in the hinterland and look for picturesque villages or striking antiquities, but all around was flat and featureless. One had to drive as far as Suffolk to get the faintest undulation in the landscape, and as Nannie thought long drives upsetting to your stomachs we never quite got to Constable's Flatford Mill. Once we were only two miles short of it when she ordered the about-turn. The evenings were uneventful and I would read in my bedroom, for there were then no late restaurants in Frinton and no cinema.

Nannie enjoyed Frinton so much that she proposed it for a second summer, and I was about to fall in weakly with this idea when Max, who must have been eight by this time and knew a boring place when he saw one, went on strike and said nothing would induce him to go there again and what was the use of a sea without any fish? So, rather sadly, I planned to split forces, Nannie and you going to Frinton, Max and I to Rose Cottage, but fate intervened. Two days before I was to chauffeur you to Frinton Nannie broke her leg and had to go to hospital. I spent the next fortnight on the road driving between Frinton (where I had deposited you with a friendly family) Rose Cottage (where Max was terrorizing the village) and London (where Nannie was not liking the hospital food and could I buy her an extra nightdress).

It was my last attempt at Frinton and even Nannie felt it was time for a change. She had heard on the nanny grapevine that 'Frinton isn't what it was – not the same class of person.' In fact, the old-fashioned nannies were already declining in number and their successors were young, skittish girls who knew all about Greek salads and skuba-diving and wanted to holiday, abroad. Nannie told me later that I had made a mistake in going to a hotel. I would have found more to occupy me if I had taken a house and we would all have enjoyed shopping and cooking and having friends to tea just as though we were at home. Well, possibly.

The Mystique of Fleet Street

I left *Harper's Bazaar* because I wanted some rest and another baby, and I conceived you almost at once. 'It's stop-go like a bus,' said an envious friend, who was having difficulty in getting pregnant. I worked through this period as a freelance and wrote my first book, *In the Mink*, finishing the last chapter as the taxi drew up at the flat to take me to King's College Hospital to give birth. I had known Michael Joseph for some time – he was publishing *Cork on the Water*, the first of your father's thrillers – and he had already approved an outline of *In the Mink*. I sent him the manuscript as soon as I arrived back at the flat bearing you in my arms, and he accepted it. I am sorry to tell you that you were not such a bouncing child as Max, but a little fretful at first, though not for long. 'Those hospitals don't know a thing about babies, they ought to be closed down,' said Nannie, who favoured home confinements.

In the Mink which, as you will remember, was about the fashion business, caused a mild stir when it was published in 1952, and was widely reviewed, for the most part favourably, though I remember one notice by the theatre critic Harold Hobson, denouncing a few harmless comments on sexual behaviour in the fashion world as shocking and disgraceful. Apart from gratifying sales, the book had one result which was to be important to me, for it drew the attention of newspaper editors to my writing, and early in 1953 I was asked at alarmingly short notice to write an article for the *Sunday Express* about Queen Mary, who had just died. Harold Keeble was then the editor, who liked the article and commissioned some more, and later in the year hired me to fill a page every Sunday called 'The Anne Scott-James Page'. The subjects were to be angled towards women, but in practice I could write about almost anything I liked.

I cannot overstress the pleasure of being a star writer on a successful newspaper. The Beaverbrook Press in those days, when Lord Beaverbrook was still alive and a hyperactive proprietor, had a mystique which impressed all journalists except those who could not stomach Beaverbrook's mischievous, but to my mind harmless, because lunatic, politics. His newspapers were clever and entertaining, with first-class writers, correspondents, cartoonists and sub-editors and an enviable standard of photography, typography and production, and unless you were a political writer, when you were directly under the Old Man's orders, you were remarkably free. I never had a word altered in seven years without a sub-editor consulting me first, sometimes ringing me at home late at night. One rule, however, all journalists must respect, and that is 'house style', a limited number of words and usages peculiar to a publishing house. If there is a word which I dislike more than most it is the arch 'undies' for 'underclothes', but when I protested at finding 'undies' on my page the sub-editor said laconically, 'It's the house style.'

Harold Keeble was a paragon as an impresario. He was one of a number of famous journalists who came to London from Yorkshire, a short, rotund man with a carefully cultivated air of childlike candour and large blue eyes which looked you full in the face while he shamelessly told you some thumping lie. He was brilliantly creative, a fount of sparkling ideas for features, in a class of his own at making up a page and writing headlines, and so witty that one was always laughing. But he was one of nature's mischief-makers – a favourite conversational gambit was 'I was defending you last night' – and profoundly treacherous. When he told you, 'I've told Tom to give you all his time in Rome and to meet you with a car and cash', you could be pretty sure that he had telephoned Tom in Rome to say, 'Don't let Anne bother you when she comes out, let her do her own work.' I once said to Anne Edwards, my opposite number on the *Daily Express*, 'If I saw Harold drowning in a pond and I had a pole I wouldn't fish him out', and she said 'I'd push him under.' That was the effect he had on many of his staff, especially the women, who were hurt by his duplicity, which the men, who were more cynical, shrugged off as part of the job.

Harold made life so entertaining that I looked forward to every day in the office. He was an eleventh-hour journalist who got his best ideas when it was almost too late and would tear up a page when it was in the press and re-make it, always for the better, so that one was rushed and scrambled. But I found I wrote better with a threatening deadline, which concentrates the mind wonderfully and makes the adrenalin flow. You will say, dear Clare, that in my working life I craved excitement. Well, so I did. So do you, for that matter, in yours. So, with double intensity, does Max. But to offset my liking for ferment in Fleet Street, I have always actively disliked a crowded social life, and love to be quiet at home, and must have time to read. When you and Max were small, I often took a taxi home instead of lunching with business friends in a restaurant to join you for a fish-and-steamed-pudding family meal in the nursery.

The work on a newspaper, though highly competitive, never scared me, because I was an old hand of nearly forty with an editorship behind me when I joined the *Sunday Express*. It is a good idea to learn the ropes of journalism on a magazine before joining a newspaper, where nobody has time to teach you. Having learned those ropes, I think a newspaper is journalistic heaven. The facilities are vast, the contacts high-powered, the opportunities for seeing the world infinite, and you do not have to niggle all the time about spending money. This is in no way an obsession of mine, and in fact I did not make a lot of money out of Fleet Street, but you cannot imagine how it lessens the strain of working under pressure to know that plane seats, cars and hotels are always there for the hiring and that stringers (local correspondents) are usually on tap. Not that I was a splashy spender – the solitary occasion when I took a suite instead of a room in a hotel was when the only accommodation available in Vienna at the time of the Hungarian uprising against Russia was a fine set of rooms just vacated by the famous foreign correspondent, Sefton Delmer, whose spending habits were notorious and were in the end, I think, his undoing.

My routine on the *Sunday Express* fitted in perfectly with my domestic life, or so I thought, though Max said later that he would have preferred a mother who had no career. I was never so happy with the non-stop turmoil of the *Daily Express*, where I spent one year, at a later date as a full-time executive, and I would recommend Sunday papers to all women journalists with children.

In the early days of each week I would take it easy, organize the household and family affairs, turn over ideas for my page, which consisted of one leading feature each week and two or three minor ones, and arrange my illustrations. On Thursday and Friday I worked long hours, writing and seeing my page to press, which would take me up to 10.00 p.m. on a Friday while I waited for a proof to take home with me. This was when I stopped being a water drinker and took to the occasional gin-and-tonic, corrupted by the subs, with whom I would spend the waiting-time in a pub. Today, with electronic printing, few journalists see a proof of what they have written, which I could not endure, for I am comma crazy.

I feel truly sorry for newspaper journalists who have never known the camaraderie of Fleet Street. It was a casualty of the dispersal of newspapers (essential if the power of the unions was to be beaten) from their traditional homes in and round Fleet Street to faraway, unfriendly sites in genteel Kensington or down the River Thames. Many young journalists, especially the new breed of freelances who fax their copy from home, have never smelt the printer's ink of the composing room, gobbled a quick lunch in a Fleet Street tavern crowded with friends from a dozen newspapers, or run into some mad-eyed editor in a corridor who stops for a chat out of which springs impromptu the idea of the day. I was getting into the lift at the *Daily Express* one evening on my way home when Harold Keeble, then on the *Daily*, seized me by the coat collar and said, 'You'll do. Princess Margaret has got engaged to a photographer called Tony Armstrong-Jones. You know him, don't you? You can write the leader page piece on it, you've got all of fifty minutes.'

Obviously I am hopelessly out-of-date in my dread of modern newspaper technology. It must be a huge advantage to word-process your copy from anywhere in the world instead of telephoning every word or trying to find a cable office. And yet, when you are alone and far from home, it can be comforting to hear the familiar voice of a telephone copytaker in London and to have a friendly word with him before starting to dictate, and the skill and accuracy of those men on what might be a faint or crackling line were beyond praise. Is it the nostalgia of retirement which makes me think that I had the best of Fleet Street? Or, when the newspapers scattered, did some of the community spirit go too?

The Formidable Nancy Mitford

Many of the lead features in my *Sunday Express page* consisted of interviews. In April, 1956, Nancy Mitford's serio-comic essay on U and non-U, which had caused much amusement and controversy among the chattering classes, was about to be published in book form under the title *Noblesse Oblige*. It seemed a good idea to telephone her at her home in Paris to ask if I might interview her for further elucidation on U, or upper-class, behaviour. She said, 'Yes, come tomorrow afternoon', so next morning off I flew.

Knowing that she was an international arbiter of taste and fashion, sharp-tongued and critical and a tormentor of the weak, I fortified myself with an excellent lunch at the Ritz, changed into a fresh shirt, rubbed up my shoes with a duster, put on clean gloves and, worrying a bit about my vowel sounds, went off to pay my call. I found a tall, slender, handsome woman with crisp dark hair and grey eyes, elegantly dressed in a white wool blouse and black skirt of unmistakably Parisian cut, friendly, but frightening – all the Mitford girls had a natural *hauteur* and clear, commanding voices. Her drawing-room was charmingly furnished with Sheraton furniture and Chinese screens and porcelain lamps and looked on to a pretty but melancholy little garden which was all trees and ivy in the French manner, nothing so vulgar as flowers.

I asked her if she would add something to the fascinating examples of U and non-U which she had instanced in her essay. This had been mostly about U language, with only an occasional tip about manners – for instance, a man when drunk might forgivably become amorous or maudlin or might even be sick, but he must not be truculent – and after careful consideration she proclaimed three stigmata which would place a person firmly in a low social bracket: trousers for women, combing the hair in public, and using anything in plastic.

I asked, 'If you are not born U, can you become U?'

'Possibly, if you go to Eton.'

'But if you are too old for school or are a girl?'

'Your chances are small.'

'Can a person of great personality transcend these standards?'

'Oh yes, for instance the late Lord Beauchamp would only drink champagne our of a jug, which would be offensive in a lesser man.'

'Don't you think that U-usage changes? Could one not today refer to corsets instead of stays, which sounds very old-world? You love all things French, and the French for a staymaker is a *corsetière*.'

'Absolutely not. It would make me shudder.'

I grasped the nettle. 'Is my behaviour U?'

She thought for a long time, for she had no wish to hurt me, only to tease, a favourite Mitford word. 'You have U legs,' she said kindly.

'How seriously do you take this whole subject?' She said not seriously at all, it was a small joke which had snowballed, but I didn't quite believe her. The only circle Nancy Mitford knew was an aristocratic clique, leavened with clever, often homosexual, writers and artists, and she was bored by anyone who did not belong – even minor characters in her books were nannies, butlers, grooms or other upper-class appendages. Perhaps this limitation of human contact was the reason why so many of the six Mitford girls went off the rails politically, with Unity and Diana fanatical for Hitler; they understood nobody outside their own set. I did not press the point, and we talked for a while about eccentric behaviour, the history of etiquette, and French versus English manners, then I thanked her for seeing me, and hurried off to catch my plane.

I had to telephone her the following afternoon to check some small point and she told me she had been lunching with Diana Cooper who told her, 'You were *mad* to see her, she'll make mincemeat of you.' She had replied, 'But she had such charm', to which Diana Cooper answered, 'They're always the worst.' However, the interview in the *Sunday Express* cannot have displeased her, for she sent me a postcard saying, 'My, you were kind.' I think she liked my polite words about her clothes, for she had an obsession with fashion and wore New Look suits, Dior originals, not copies, for she hated cheap clothes. But even in her Dior model, she looked incurably English.

I did not meet her again until years later after I had married Osbert, who took us both to dinner at the Garrick Club. I have never felt such a gooseberry. Osbert had known Nancy since girlhood and had been a guest at her wedding in 1933 to the ineffable Peter Rodd, and was at home in her world, which I was not, and knew all the jokes and teases. The two of them rattled away throughout the evening and ignored me completely (U behaviour, I suppose), so I ate and drank in silence and listened, half rapt and half revolted, to their sparkling conversation. Nancy Mitford was a formidable lady, and very, very clever, whose tragedy it was to make a joke of everything, for as the years went by and husband, lover and health all failed her, many of the jokes turned sour.

Naked in Moscow

I was sitting at my typewriter in my bedroom in the Hotel Metropole, Moscow, wearing nothing but a bra and briefs, for it was boiling hot, when the door burst open and a burly but smartly dressed Russian came in without knocking. He did not retreat or apologize, but greeted me effusively in bad French, saying that he had got my letter. He was a distinguished scientist to whom I had been given a letter of introduction by a geologist friend in London who had met him at a conference, and I had posted the letter without much hope of response, just for luck. I was now in a social dilemma. Should I go into the bathroom and put on my dressing-gown or continue to chat in a nonchalant manner? As my new friend was in full conversational flow and did not seem at all put out by my semi-nudity I chose the latter course.

I was in Moscow in June 1956 to write some articles for the *Sunday Express*, and as we were then in the deep-freeze compartment of the cold war contact with Russians other than interpreters and petty officials was not at all easy. But my new friend was high enough up in the hierarchy to mix with foreigners, and he invited me to spend the following Sunday at his family dacha in the country, promising to send his chauffeur to fetch me. What a break.

Even the laziest private traveller has ambitions to get under the skin of a foreign country by entering local life, even if his contact is brief and superficial. For a journalist, every insight is not merely agreeable but professionally important. Every newspaper reader or TV viewer at that time knew the same bald facts about Russian politics and economics, but many looked to the likes of me for something more human, for a picture of everyday Russian life. For instance, a seemingly slight, but deeply revealing, remark was made by my guide in one of the three cathedrals of the Kremlin as we looked at a beautiful twelfth-century ikon of the Madonna. 'That is the mother of Christ, you have heard of her, I expect?' On this assignment I had already taken tea with a poor family in their almost slummy flat, elderly educated people who had come far down in the world to live in unprivileged squalor. (Again, an introduction from a London friend given on condition I published no names). Now I was to spend a day with a prosperous professional family

A large chauffeur-driven car arrived as promised on Sunday and I was driven away from the heart of Moscow, dominated by the lovely onion domes of the cathedrals, through the grim concrete suburbs, into the country. We drove for perhaps thirty miles through a flat landscape, passing no real villages, just clumps of shacks, and no inns or cafés (the traveller in Russia must take his own food), to my friend's dacha, a substantial wooden house in a forest of birch and pine trees. I learned that he and his wife used it for weekends and had an apartment in the city.

Our day was spent much like a Sunday in the country at home. On arrival my host introduced me to his wife, who was a pretty woman, much slimmer than the chunky women you see all over Moscow, most of whom are dwarfs, and we all had a glass of tea and then drove to see the local 'stately home', a former palace of the Youssoupoffs which had been converted into a museum. On our return we walked in the woods and picked lilies-of-the-valley for me to take back to my hotel, for there were few flowers to buy in Moscow, the flower-stalls being gaudy with paper flowers. Then we had a cold lunch, with a variety of dishes which were hospitably pressed on me, but it was sparse by our standards – sardines, cucumbers, bits and pieces of meat, bread, cake and tea.

The talk was anodyne. My political questions got no further than, 'With goodwill on both sides our countries can get on together.' Questions on standards of living were oiled over with, 'Everyone has enough food and clothing but we want more goods in the shops.' On questions of freedom my host's French dried up. At that time a Russian could not travel even inside Russia without a permit.

With my hostess, a university teacher, it was easier. She told me they were thinking of moving house because the land round their dacha, which they had chosen for its rural peace, was being developed. The servant shortage was growing acute. They spent their holidays on the Black Sea, she, unlike her husband, never having been abroad. One of their luxuries was a well-loved Scottie terrier, the only pet animal I had seen in or near Moscow.

Before I left, my host promised to get me a ticket for the Bolshoi ballet and a much-needed place on a flight to Leningrad for which I had been struggling in vain with Intourist, getting no further than a ghostly waiting list. Both tickets arrived the next morning, and I was able to steal two days away from my work to see that incomparable city and the Hermitage Museum.

I loved my Russian assignment. I saw much that was beautiful, much that was amusing, much that was ugly, but everything was excitingly novel. There was sometimes a faint tinge of anxiety, as when I arrived in Leningrad at midnight to find nobody to meet me, and the airport was closing down.

In Russia every tiny success was a joy because it was so difficult to achieve. I have been alone in many cities with a column to claw out of the air, but there were always stringers, facilities and friends available, and no assignment has given me such a sense of adventure as Moscow in 1956.

A Skirmish with the Laws of Libel

Though not averse to controversy, I have not often brushed with the laws of libel, on only three occasions, to be precise. My baptism was on *Picture Post*, when I was misled by a pamphlet of highly respectable origins which attacked the reactionary Council of the Zoological Society. My argument was probably correct and the libel doubtful, but we received a writ. The *Picture Post* management took it calmly and a small sum was paid out of court.

The second was sheer carelessness. In the *Sunday Express* I referred to a peeress of the realm as a widow, but her husband was very much alive and prominent in public life. The peer was a friend of Lord Beaverbrook and it was common practice for a man or woman aggrieved at something written for an *Express* newspaper to telephone the editor and begin with the menacing words, 'I am a close friend of Lord Beaverbrook.' But this lady rang me personally more in sorrow than in anger and was extremely nice about it, and I published an apology from the heart, for I must have caused her some distress.

The third occasion was more serious. The natural childbirth cult, headed by Dr Grantly Dick Read, was in its prime, and I wrote a trenchant piece criticizing, not natural childbirth, which suits many mothers, but the mumbo-jumbo which went with it under Dr Read's auspices. There was a strong element of exhibitionism, with some women recording their deliveries and replaying or writing about them in the newspapers pang by pang and puff by puff. 'The fearless woman', wrote Dr Read, 'advances to the dais of the Almighty to receive the prize for her accomplishment. She does nor cringe in anticipation of admonition, but is proud and grateful for her just reward.' Unfair, I thought, on the poor mother who opted for a painkiller.

There are many satisfactory ways to have a baby – with or without an anaesthetic, in hospital or at home, with your husband present or drinking at his club, taking maternity leave or working to the last, joining a group for pregnancy or handling it alone – but I was offended by the moral superiority claimed by the followers of Dr Read. The fearless woman who refuses all painkilling aids certainly deserves congratulations, but so do we all, and I felt that in overselling painless childbirth Dr Read was misleading many innocent women who, expecting the baby to slide out quietly while they relaxed and took deep breaths, might meet with an unpleasant shock. And I thought it cruel to induce guilt in a mother who asked for an anaesthetic.

I argued my case fairly, I thought, but somehow the word 'quackery' crept into my column and the stand-in lawyer who was taking the place of our usual hawk-eyed libel reader let it pass, and we received a heavy writ from Dr Read.

I was rescued by the unlikely medium of television. The BBC wanted Dr Read and myself to take part in a discussion programme about natural childbirth, and they would not screen it if a libel case was pending. So anxious was Dr Read to appear on television that he settled within days for a small sum of money, and the programme came on live, the two of us glaring at one another with intense dislike.

Even if the *Express* had had to pay up heavily and grovel with apology it wouldn't have hurt them much, or perhaps they would have fought the case, which would have involved me in hideous waste of time. The laws of libel are muddled, juries chancy, and judges unpredictable in this area and not inclined to favour newspapers, so I got out of it lightly. I was rewarded by hundreds of letters from women thanking me for speaking up on their behalf.

In a Primeval World

One of the pleasures of journalism is that you can land up anywhere, and in 1960 I found myself camping in Kenya beside a sand river fringed with palms to which herds of elephants made their slow, deliberate way down from the hills in the evening to drink and spend the night. A few weeks earlier I had 'crossed the street', which, when most newspaper offices were clumped round Fleet Street, meant moving from one newspaper to another. I had joined the *Daily Mail* as a weekly columnist on general subjects, the huge advantage being that I would at last be wholly free from the trammels of women's journalism, and my column would appear on the leader page.

Crossing the street was not such a traumatic experience as you might think, for it was happening all the time, and the proprietors were as erratic in their own way as the employees. Most of the editors I worked for on *Express* newspapers, including Harold Keeble and Ted (now Sir Edward) Pickering, had been at some time on the *Daily Mail*, Ted later left the *Express* for the *Mirror*, and later again for *The Times*, Robert Edwards left the *Express* to join the *Mirror* Group, Keeble went back to the *Mail*, where the present chairman, Sir David English, was formerly on the *Express*, as was the *Daily Mail* columnist, John Junor. It was all something of a parlour game, and I don't think even the proprietors felt much resentment about it. I myself never deserted an editor who had hired me, but so frequent were the editorial changes when Lord Beaverbrook was the supremo that you might say to an editor, 'Goodnight, see you in the morning' to find he had been promoted/demoted/transferred/sacked overnight – at one later period the *Daily Express* had five editors in ten years. I had been hired on the *Sunday Express* by Harold Keeble, who was replaced after a year by John Junor. After a further three years I went for a brief spell to the *Daily Mail*'s sister paper, the *Sunday Dispatch*, for a lot more money, was bought back by the *Daily Express* to be Women's Adviser to Beaverbrook Newspapers, which I did not enjoy, for male chauvinism was rife, and female executives were firmly crushed, and settled into the *Daily Mail* for a very happy eight years in 1960. The *Daily Mail* was then a broadsheet newspaper, not a tabloid, and was more serious in content than it is now, or at least there was scope for longer articles.

My new editor, Bill Hardcastle, wanted me to begin not with a single column, but with a series of articles to make a bit of a splash, and I had suggested exploring the wildlife of Africa. Anxiety for the future of wild animals was already awakening, good wildlife stories were sure of a readership, and the subject was agreed. So I flew to Nairobi and arranged to join two different safaris, one a working safari, accompanying a game warden on his round of duties in the bush, the other a hunting safari with one of the last of the white hunters, a man who had shot big game with Ernest Hemingway, whom, by the way, he intensely disliked, describing him as 'yellow'. A local wildlife photographer, Ted Mullins, had already been signed up to travel with me, a young man who flew a two-seater Piper Cruiser plane, so that we could reach the remotest places in the bush. Kenya was not yet independent and the abundant wildlife was protected by a magnificent team of game wardens. The terrible losses, particularly of elephant, now poached almost to extinction in some districts, was still in the future.

After a day spent making my arrangements and having a safari suit made in which I felt I could have held my own with the sirens of the Happy Valley set, I set off with Ted at dawn on a bumpy two-hour flight over a primeval world of virgin forests and extinct volcanoes to Tsavo, a vast tract of bush country in southern Kenya. The plane felt very small.

We were met at the landing strip by a game warden called David Sheldrick, who was said to know more about elephants than any man alive and kept elephants at home as pets, and who could sense, before he saw it, every living presence in the bush, and could interpret every sound – or silence. He had once been a white hunter but had grown sick of animal slaughter and turned to preservation. After explaining our mission, which was to make a photo-reportage of the wildlife of the bush, we set off on a day-long drive to the sand river where we were to make our first night's camp. David, Ted and I, with two black rangers in dashing Beau Geste uniforms, travelled in a Land Rover, followed by a lorry with six African boys and our gear, for you do not travel with only one vehicle in the bush. For hours we bumped and hurtled over rocky tracks through a hot red landscape, for the red dust of Tsavo rises in the dry season to smother the bushes and trees and even the animals.

For David this was a routine working trip, and we stopped from time to time while he checked the movements of game, watched the water supply, inspected the occasional corpse of an animal, pin-pointed by circling vultures, to see what it had died of, and laid his plans to catch poachers, who were slaughtering thousands of wild animals every year. The bush was alive with wonderful creatures – giraffe, elephant, hippo, tortoise, buffalo, rhino, zebra, deer, the occasional lion or scarcer leopard, and many beautiful birds. At first I was very slow to spot them and I missed the only leopard of the day. 'You must look *into* the bush, not *at* the bush', David told me, and in time I did get a little keener-sighted. Sometimes we left the Land Rover and took a walk of inspection, and I asked David why he did not take his gun. He told me that most large animals, when they smell humans, will turf off. This is their world, and you must not approach it aggressively. I realized that I was there by courtesy of the animals, and felt apologetic for my intrusion into their ancient ways.

It was nearly dark when we reached the sand river and got out and rested while the boys set up camp, which turned out to be like a three-star hotel. Out of the lorry came a series of fitted, numbered cases which contained three sleeping tents for us, a mess tent and a tent for the boys, camp beds and stools and folding tables, table-cloths, a battery of cooking utensils, crockery, food and soft drinks, linen, glass, mosquito nets, a sprinkler for a shower bath and a bamboo bath-mat, a flat-iron, washbowls, soap, towels, bedside lamps and even a paraffin refrigerator. 'I'm afraid you have taken a lot of extra trouble for me', I said, but David said no, he spent most of his life in the bush and he liked to be comfortable.

When the sprinkler was set up I went to take a shower, but what with a huge green spider on the bath-mat and elephants trumpeting two hundred yards away, I felt that this was no place to take off all one's clothes, so I washed off the red dust which coated me as best I could, put on a clean shirt, earrings and some scent as my contribution to the fine old British tradition of dressing for dinner in the jungle, and was ready for our meal. There were five courses, including paw-paw with lemon, beef, and asparagus with melted butter, which David assured me was quite a normal safari menu.

After dinner, we sat through the evening listening to the dying fall of the bush, which became ever quieter until the calm sank into extreme silence. At night the animals rarely trumpet or roar; there is an occasional snuffling or snorting, perhaps the baying of a hyena or the purring of a lion. There was a little moonlight that night, and across the river I could just make out some flapping ears and weaving trunks. After a while I went to my tent and fell dead asleep.

When I woke the horizon was green and the palm-trees across the river showed in black silhouette. Then the green turned to gold, the silence began to break as waking birds piped and twittered, baboons caterwauled in the trees, and a pair of squawking parrots flew over the camp. The elephants shuffled off into the bush, with some rhino which had joined them in the night. A new day for the animals had begun.

Three days later I was on my second safari, this time on a hunting safari in the mountainous bush country of Tanzania, but after Tsavo, where we had been fellow inhabitants with the animals in their wild world, it was an anti-climax, indeed distasteful to me. I went because I wanted to look at wildlife from another viewpoint, and a party of American oil millionaires and their wives had generously allowed me to join their enormously expensive expedition, but I did not enjoy it.

These trips were already in their decline and the white hunters were fed up with them. Shorn of the danger which gave zest to the more primitive hunting expeditions earlier in the century, they bore little relation to sport. The white hunter in charge virtually placed the big game in position for the hunter to shoot, and when one of the women in the party shot a standing buffalo and wounded it, leaving it for the hunter to follow into the bush and kill, and was then photographed standing on the body grasping the trophy, I felt sick. I was glad when it was time to leave the hunting party and climb into our little plane to fly back to Nairobi.

In spite of this un-idyllic episode, I left Nairobi for London in a state of elation. There cannot be many professions which pay for you to roam through Africa with a pencil and notebook looking at lions and birds.

Joy Adamson

My trip to Africa was not, of course, a mere matter of swanning around enjoying the scenery. I had to find a diversity of stories and I thought it would vary the pace if I visited Joy Adamson, a controversial figure in Kenya who had reared a wild lioness cub which she named Elsa, and written the bestseller, *Born Free*. Joy, who was Austrian by birth, had been sanctified by readers in Britain and the United States as a gentle, almost mystical sort of woman who could charm the wild beasts and birds like St Joan of Arc or St Francis of Assisi.

This was, I found, a portrait in pastel. Joy was very, very tough, dynamic, ambitious and egotistical, and widely disliked in Kenya. This was partly jealousy on the part of the numerous Kenyans who had themselves reared lion cubs but had not had the wit to cash in on their exploits. It was partly because animal-lovers said that humanizing a lion wasn't fair on the beast, which would be alienated from its kind when it returned to the bush. It was partly distaste for her passion for publicity. To make my own judgement I drove with my photographer, Ted Mullins, to Joy's home forty-five miles north of the equator in the semi-desert country of the Northern Frontier Province, where her husband, George Adamson, was game warden, overseeing a territory of 120,000 square miles which extended to Ethiopia. I enjoyed meeting Joy and admired her intimate knowledge of the bush, and its animals and plants, but I found it hard to like her, for she sold herself too hard. Every sentence began with 'I'.

Joy and George lived in a stone bungalow in the heart of a burnt-up country dotted with thorn bushes from which the nests of weaver-birds hung like Christmas-tree decorations. The bungalow was delightful. Outside, the house was covered with flowering shrubs and there was a pool in the unfenced garden where mongooses, porcupines, or sometimes a lion or elephant would come in the evening to drink.

Inside, I was struck by symbols of the weird paradox of the white African attitude to animals, that the hunter loves what he kills, for there were zebra-covered chairs and a lion-skin on one wall, a shock when one remembered all those photographs of Joy cuddling, kissing and playing games with her bottle-fed lioness. Was this Elsa? I had the tact not to ask. I soon learned that Elsa had grown up and had three cubs herself, which she had taken off into the bush 150 miles away. Other walls were hung with botanical drawings by Joy, who was a gifted artist, and with sketches of African tribes in ceremonial dress, because she was also something of an anthropologist, and knew the meaning of every feather and fetish.

Joy was a leathery-looking, beady-eyed lady, but highly hospitable, who welcomed us with an excellent lunch, after which she took us for a drive in her Land Rover through the bush, a truly knowledgeable guide, expert on pug-marks and droppings. Of all the wild creatures she showed us, the birds were the greatest wonder, including larger birds than I had seen in Tsavo. There were secretary birds, which are eccentric eagles with quills on the neck and a solemn, judicial walk; many crested cranes, which perform a love dance; marabou storks, carrion birds which cannot tear their meat, so they attack vultures and snatch the morsels they disgorge; and fast-trotting ostriches, birds one had loved so well in the nursery.

Back in the bungalow, I asked her about her attitude to animals in general and Elsa in particular.

'I have shot just about everything in my time, including elephant,' she told me, 'but I do not shoot any more now that the game is growing scarce. Elsa has gone away, but I go on safari every fortnight to visit her, taking a present of goats. Elsa is still tame with me, but less so with George, and her cubs have not inherited her human fixation.' Cynics in Nairobi foretold, not without relish, that sooner or later Elsa would revert to her animal nature and finish off Joy. This did not happen, but some time after I left Africa Elsa was found dead in the bush, and the cause of death was not ascertained – the stories were contradictory. Some said she was caught in a poacher's trap, others that she was killed as an alien by other lions.

I do not know what motivated Joy to spend her adult life in the wild. Great travellers have been inspired by different longings. Some have wished to dominate the wild. Scientific curiosity has spurred the naturalists and history the archaeologists. A taste for strange people and places has sent many men and women, from A.W. Kinglake to Wilfred Thesiger, from Lady Hester Stanhope to Freya Stark, to live in the near east. Religion inspired the French missionaries in China and a streak of mysticism has sent pilgrims into solitude to learn to know themselves. I asked Joy if she would ever return to live in her native country, but she said no. 'I am a person who needs total freedom and infinite space. I hate too many people around me.' It seemed a good enough reason.

How I Fell Among Billionaires

It was Max who lured me there in 1967 when he was touring the United States on a young journalist's scholarship. In a middle-west state which I will not name he was the guest for some weeks of a hugely rich family with more money than sense, and feeling homesick he wrote imploring me to visit him. His hostess would be happy to put me up. As I was just then arranging a tour of north America for the *Daily Mail*, it was easy to fit in an extra stop, and it was sheer bad luck that Max had fallen in love with a local girl two days before I arrived and had little time for me. That's motherhood.

His defection left me in the hands of an incalculably rich couple called Tommy and Bella who greeted me effusively on my arrival, but over three days never learned my name. They were rarely at home, and then were mostly on the telephone, but Bella told me kindly, 'Just find your way around, there's food in the ice-box and take any of the cars.'

The house was a neo-Georgian mansion out in the country, or what passes for country in America, where every lane has curbstone edges, in a fine position overlooking a lake. It teemed with gadgets, from automated garage doors which opened as your car approached to a kitchen with cooked food always at the ready in thermostatically controlled containers. There was a well-stocked cocktail bar with life-size dummies of soldiers in red uniforms and busbies sitting on two of the bar stools. There were crinoline ladies over every telephone. In Tommy's den there were three television sets piled on top of each other so that he could watch three football games at once. The only thing lacking was home comfort. My bedroom was icy because the central heating gave up in the guest wing, though for consolation there was a Gideon Bible by my bed. As at Southfork Ranch in *Dallas*, nobody ever seemed to cook anything, but snackbar food was always ready and you could knock up fried chicken or hamburgers in a jiffy. The only servant was Jessie, a pathetic little maid-of-all-work with a hole-in-the-heart condition who should have been in nursing care. Jessie told me that she was dying, but, though often tired, she was perfectly happy, looking forward to kneeling to Jesus and seeing the bright angels with their beautiful wings. Her vision of heaven was multi-coloured and corporeal, her faith unruffled by doubt, for this was the Bible belt of America beyond which she had never travelled. Her doctor had told her that the cold climate would be fatal to her and she should move to the south, but she could not afford it. She died a year later.

Of course I had always known that great wealth carries its burdens – intense competition, study of the markets, board meetings, staff management, administrative toil and that sort of thing – but I had not appreciated the day-to-day effort involved in simply getting rid of the stuff. Tommy did not seem too bothered by his money; he had his sporting interests and his club, his cars and his plane, but Bella nearly killed herself shopping. Every morning she left the house early with a station wagon and drove thirty miles to the city to spend for dear life, buying she knew not what, dresses, furs, furniture, gadgets, novelties from heart-shaped pillows to monkey-band figurines. These would be gift-wrapped while she lunched with women friends, then loaded by the store commissionaires into the car, which Bella would drive thirty miles home again, and then unpack the parcels herself and pile them into a spare room the size of a small warehouse. It was intensive work.

On my first morning, my hosts went out early (Max had disappeared), and as I was suffering from jet lag I thought I would take a walk round the lake to clear my head, but the lake was private property and fenced in with barbed wire, with no lakeside path or access for a stranger. I tried walking along the residential streets near by, but ferocious dogs barking in every garden scared me back to the house. I was now a worried woman, I must get on with some work, I must get away from this awful hole to the city, above all, *I must find Max.* I was making coffee when the dear boy telephoned to say that he had organized my life, worked out some good stories, made me three appointments and arranged a dinner party in the university. If I would take a taxi into the city he would meet me and brief me.

With Max's help I worked for a couple of days and cabled my column to London, then caught a plane to my next stop, Detroit, which I had never thought of as a home-from-home, but which turned out to be positively cosy compared with the cheerless suburbia I had left.

I don't mean to suggest that Tommy and Bella did no good with their money. Tommy, who owned a football team, supported many sporting causes and Bella sat on charitable committees and contributed handsomely to the funds. They were hospitable in a frenetic way, and guests poured in and out in the evenings for whisky and cocktails, often on their way from one party and on to another. They regularly entertained overseas students in their house (of all nationalities, there was no hint of a colour bar), which was how Max came to be there, with a car at his disposal and his mother in tow. Yet I think of it as a sad house, more of a motel than a home, with no connected conversation and never a sit-down meal.

My Colleague Bernard Levin

I wrote a number of features for the *Daily Mail* before starting my weekly comment column in 1961. This was to appear every Wednesday on the leader page, with an adjacent column, which appeared daily, by Bernard Levin. I stipulated that if on a Tuesday, which I always spent writing in the office, we both wanted to pick up the same news story, I should have first choice. Bernard agreed.

Bernard never revoked on this treaty, though he would sometimes telephone me at the crack of dawn, when we were both scouring our newspapers for stories worthy of comment, to put in a claim. He once said in an unnaturally casual voice, 'You don't want the one about Hartley Shawcross, do you?' I was at that moment mentally composing a few pithy words about a misfortune which had befallen Lord Shawcross on the previous day when he was opening a new hotel in Manchester – the ceiling had fallen in on his head. I felt that he had missed a great opportunity to lambast the building trade in his speech and I was preparing some quick research on recent building delays and imbecilities. I remembered that in one new house the hand-basin had been put in before the floor was laid, so that the basin came knee-height and the family had to wash on all-fours, and that a few weeks earlier a new church had been built in Yorkshire which collapsed before it was opened, and a police-station in south London had been built back to front.

But Lord Shawcross said mildly, 'Just teething troubles' as he picked the plaster out of his hair, and went on with his prepared piece about the spirit of business enterprise ... interest in modern architecture ... Manchester the heart of Britain ... tourism needed good hotels ... and so on. 'Bernard, I have to have it', I said to the voice on the telephone, and he replied with good humour, 'It was worth a try.'

At some stage we feature writers moved out of the large open room where we had our desks and were put into smaller rooms, and I shared a room and a secretary with Bernard, a chastening experience. For whereas I often chewed my pen and hunted for words and rewrote my copy, Bernard would decide what he wanted to say, then put a sheet of paper in his typewriter and the witty words would pour forth. Sometimes he would telephone a distinguished friend for facts or opinions, and the friend always seemed to be available and to have the facts at his finger tips. Bernard was, and is, fluent but meticulous with facts, a born journalist.

I think he was only once seriously annoyed with me, and that was when I opened a packet on my desk and drew out an original Augustus John drawing – a ravishing little sketch of a nude with a nun – with a letter from John's widow, Dorelia, who had sent it from France as a present, out of the blue. Some weeks earlier I had interviewed Mr Edward Heath, and finding little of interest to say about him I mentioned in my article that I envied him the collection of John drawings on the walls of his flat. Dorelia, whom I had never met, accompanied the drawing with a charming letter saying that she had read the interview and would much rather I had the drawings than Mr Heath, so would I care for this one? I was so pleased that I was almost in tears and of course showed it to Bernard for his admiration. He was genuinely cross.

'Carole,' he said to our pretty shared secretary, 'I will dictate a letter to Mrs John on Anne's behalf to save her the trouble, are you ready? "Dear Mrs John, It is extremely kind of you to send me the delightful drawing by your late husband – as you know, I am a great admirer of his work. But unfortunately, journalists on the *Daily Mail* are not allowed to accept perquisites, and I must regretfully send it back." ' 'Carole,' I said, 'ignore Bernard's pleasantries; I will be writing my letter by hand, *and I will post it myself*.' Bernard and I were not on good terms for the rest of the day.

I don't remember another cross word, except occasionally when we sent for Fowler's *English Usage* to resolve a linguistic argument. But our good relationship was largely due to my tolerance, for Bernard always treated me as a moron, to which I made no objection. He was irascible, as you would expect, but awfully amusing, always fair, and would even condescend to help me if I was seriously stuck for a story. His offering would probably be expressed in this fashion. 'Anne Scott-James, how you ever got into Fleet Street I cannot imagine, you never seem to have an idea in your head, but nonetheless, I do not like to see a woman in distress without lifting a finger to help her, and I would commend you to page five of today's *Financial Times*, which you are too featherpated to read, where there is a promising paragraph about the new industry of breeding miniature fish for fish fingers.' 'Thank you', I would say humbly, as I turned to the *Financial Times*.

The Craft of the Columnist

I wrote a column for about fifteen years altogether, first for the *Sunday Express* and later for the *Daily Mail*, but I don't want to write about my own column. I am thinking about the column as a craft – I mean the personal column in which the lucky journalist 'airs his views', not the informative specialist column on, say, sport or finance, which is quite a different animal.

The personal column is designed not so much to inform as to provoke a lively reaction in the reader's mind, and though such columns proliferate in today's newspapers and weekly journals, very few make much of a mark. This is partly because there are too many columns – a Sunday newspaper may have five men and women pontificating on the same day on female circumcision or the Booker Prize, or whatever is the topic of the week – but it is also because writing a column is not as easy as it looks. Journalists who are first-class in other fields, perhaps as leader-writers or investigative reporters, may fail when they attempt a personal column because their style is too portentous, or their chosen subjects too abstruse, or because they use their space to feed their vanity. Writing a column can enlarge the susceptible ego.

Though every columnist has his or her own methods, I feel that a good column must have two qualities – it must be hotly topical and it must be lucid and tightly constructed. It does not matter whether the reader agrees or disagrees with the views expressed – the more controversy, the better – so long as they strike a chord in the reader's mind. He says to himself, 'He is dead right about illiteracy, a youngster came into my office yesterday who couldn't spell "cat"', or, 'Just what my wife was saying about factory chickens', or 'Buttering up the Prime Minister – he must be mad or paid to do it.'

Most columnists would agree about the technical approach to their business, giving high priority to the art of 'keeping in touch'. But genius can transcend the rules, and one of the great columnists of our time, the late William Connor of the *Daily Mirror*, who wrote as 'Cassandra', broke many of them. He was that rare bird, an armchair columnist. He did not circulate among influential people, a necessary stimulant and source of ideas for most of us, but read and read, and chose his subjects from his reading. His social life was not spent at Westminster or the Ritz, but drinking with his cronies in pubs near Fleet Street or his home. He read over breakfast, he read in the train, he read the news reports when he arrived at the office. He read books, he read English newspapers and magazines, he read the foreign press, he read advertisements and handouts, he even read children's comics, and from all this reading he distilled two or three perceptive and witty paragraphs not once a week, but every day. However, if a novice attempted to imitate this stay-at-home routine, he would probably end up with a leisurely essay in the style of Charles Lamb.

For the rest of us the bones of a column must be sought in a more active way. Few journalists work well in isolation, and much of a columnist's time is spent in circulating. If he (or she, some of the best columnists are women) is established, he will have good contacts among the great and the good, and they will provide background information and possibly scoops. If he has not become over-addicted, as many do, to high-class society, he will also tap the ideas of lesser mortals, for a bus conductor or fellow golfer may well reveal how the wind of public opinion is blowing. He will travel anywhere at any time if a promising story beckons him away from his patch. It goes without saying that he will read the newspapers very thoroughly and keep an eye on television. I think that most columnists live with their column all the time, eyes and ears open for a significant incident, or just a good joke.

I personally believe that many journalists today write so many columns in a week that they have not enough material to go round, and the results are thin. Lord Beaverbrook would not allow his staff to write for other organizations, even if they were not in competition, and there might even be a fuss if one filled an occasional slot on radio or television. No doubt this was partly jealousy on his part – he liked to own the people on his payroll body and soul, hiring them as full-time, not freelance writers. But the fact that they were not spreading their talents more widely than they could bear did make sense. Today, journalists expect a high lifestyle, and it is not uncommon for a writer to publish almost identical columns in a Sunday paper, a daily paper, and a weekly magazine. This helps to pay the school fees, but at the price of a few yawns from the reader.

One other attribute which the columnist needs was accounted high by the great *Express* features editor, Harold Keeble. When asked by aspiring journalists what gift he valued most he would say 'stamina'. He meant, I think, sheer physical health as well as a capacity to pull out the stops in an emergency, for a columnist's is a rackety life.

Putting the column into words is not, to my mind, so demanding as the generating of ideas, and should not present an experienced journalist with much difficulty. The writing must be succinct and must go straight to the point, even if the words are occasionally abstruse – I am not arguing for prose for children. It should for choice be entertaining. And it must address the reader on equal terms; a columnist who wants to patronize should be writing specialist articles. Finding a good first sentence is a useful piece of technique, and one brilliant columnist with years of Fleet Street cynicism behind him once said to me, 'I like to start with a paradox and end with a platitude.'

You may have noticed that, except for my hero, Bill Connor, I have not mentioned any columnists by name, partly because it would be invidious, partly because columnists come and go. But any addict of the press will have a favourite columnist, and if my judgement is anywhere near the truth, that column will be witty, sincere, well-informed and wide-ranging. The writer will know Wigan as well as Westminster.

Mrs Thatcher and Other Contributors

On *Harper's Bazaar* and occasionally on the *Daily* or *Sunday Express* it was my job to commission articles from outside writers, who would be punctual or tardy, relaxed or hysterical, according to their natures. I have a reverence for professionalism and was not always patient with a contributor who was regularly late, thinking of the giant Victorian novelists who wrote like clockwork for serialization. Some of my experiences with contributors were memorable and I'll recall them, not in chronological or alphabetical order, certainly not in order of merit, but just as they occur to me.

Mrs Thatcher wrote an article for me in 1960 when I was editing a series on parents for the *Daily Express*. Well-known parents wrote about their attitudes to bringing up children, including Bob Monkhouse on his adopted daughter and the Revd Marcus Morris ('I'm a selfish father') on his family of four. Mrs Thatcher, the newly elected MP for Finchley, a mother of two, seemed the right sort of person to contribute, so I telephoned her to discuss it and mentioned that the fee would be £100. Her reaction was unique.

'Yes, I would like to do the article, I'll write about bringing up my daughter, who is now six, but the fee is too high. The current rate for a short article in a national newspaper is £50.'

'The editor himself fixed the fee, so you need not worry about it.'

'No, my fee is £50', so the smaller sum was settled. Her prices went up in later days, and her memoirs were sold for an alleged £3 million in 1991.

The article was delivered on time, the correct length, and so on, but was disappointingly banal. Mrs Thatcher wanted her daughter to work to a high academic standard at school, to learn manners, dress sense and cookery at home, to go to a university and to have a serious career. I could have written it in my sleep. Except on matters of economics Mrs Thatcher was never, to my mind, a woman of ideas.

John Betjeman wrote three poems for me when I edited *Harper's Bazaar*, which filled me with pride, as the magazine had never before soared into the literary stratosphere. One of these, called 'Christmas', was for a Christmas Number, and I had to have it by a certain date or it failed its purpose. Nothing makes one feel so coarse, so insensitive to the creative throes of an artist, as asking a poet to meet a deadline, but I hardened my heart and reminded John once or twice about his promise. He suffered, but he did achieve the poem, which was charming. He was, as always, diffident. 'You won't like it, old girl, it's rather religious. It's also rather long. In fact, I don't think it's any good at all. Don't feel obliged to use it. How do I look in the snaps? Such a nice photographer, I hope he took me out of focus.'

Another poem which John wrote for me, 'The Dear Old Village', was, for John, unusually savage, satirizing corrupt councillors, black-market farmers and village yobs as well as lamenting the refuse in the pond and the loss of the village school. 'You'll find it strong meat, I'm afraid, but it's a correction to all this modern adulation of rusticity.'

The most difficult contributor I ever knew was Elizabeth David. For the evocative prose, the scholar's knowledge, the imagination which turned cookery writing into literature, I would put up with almost anything, and indeed did so for a long period. But Elizabeth could never understand that there comes a moment in the birth of any publication *when it simply has to go to press*. She seemed to feel that my entire magazine existed for her contribution, that our very format should be expanded to accommodate an extra word, that she should not be asked to sacrifice a single adjective. 'Dear Elizabeth,' I would say over the telephone, 'you must either come in and cut two words yourself or let me do it, but I cannot make the page any larger.'

The reward for publishing her articles was great, for they were widely read and loved. I was her first editor – she was introduced to me by our mutual friend, Veronica Nicholson, who was on my fashion staff – and her first piece for me, in March, 1949, was called 'Rice Again', celebrating the return of rice to the shops after a long absence. Writing about *risotto* she gave a recipe 'which I took down while watching it being cooked by the *padrona* in a quay-side restaurant in Alassio', a piece of typical Elizabeth David magic by which the whole Italian scene and the fat, cheerful people of the waterfront are conjured up along with the dish. The recipe appeared later in the book which Elizabeth was writing concurrently with her articles, *A Book of*

Mediterranean Food. It was published by John Lehmann in 1950 with a beautiful jacket and illustrations by John Minton. Elizabeth and I remained friends and years later, when I was doing some research on cottagers' food, she gave me the run of her library and herself picked out the most likely books.

Lesley Blanch was of course a joy to work with as I had known her for so long. I asked her to write a short profile for *Harper's Bazaar* of Eden Box, the new Sunday painter who had taken up a brush in middle age and was painting naive pictures of jungle animals in sedate Victorian surroundings, such as a lion and a tiger lying down on a lawn where plump little children were taking tea with their nanny. Lesley indulged in the usual breast-beating ... disastrous domestic situation ... cook walked out taking the saucepans ... was herself just leaving for Samarkand ... recovering from flu, temperature of 105°F ... but she wrote a beautiful piece about Eden Box, whom she had known from childhood, called 'The Gentle Jungle'. Lesley, outwardly so scatterbrained, had a solid core.

The great and the famous were often the most good-humoured and punctilious contributors. Nobody could have been easier than Graham Sutherland with whom I once worked on a feature for *Harper's Bazaar* (rashly using a Sutherland painting of grasshoppers on the cover, which shocked the advertisers), or than John Piper when I wrote about his garden years later for *Queen.* To show the design of his garden, cut up into irregular squares and odd corners, he drew a bird's-eye sketch to go with my article, an unexpected bonus. I once commissioned an article from H.E. Bates for a section I was editing for the *Sunday Express* which was unfortunately *too* good, for the editor, Harold Keeble, pinched it for the leader page, leaving my section with a gaping hole. Elizabeth Longford was a favourite of mine, always gentle and thoughtful and ready on time, but she had had long experience as a journalist before she became famous as a historian. What was more, she always seemed pleased to be asked, whereas many contributors would take on a job as a favour.

I have a black list in my mind of contributors who did *not* fulfil their commissions and after too many defections one had to drop them. It was more often artists than writers who missed the deadline, which raises an interesting question. Is the writer more amenable to discipline than the visual artist?

A Bit of Background

As I said when I began to write these letters, I did not want them to be essays in egotism or revelations of my private life. But perhaps I have been too reticent and appear as a disembodied spirit without any background, and I ought to fill in a few facts about my home and family. You know most of it, but not quite all.

My marriage to your father lasted from 1944 for eighteen years, through all of which Max and you and our home meant much more to me than my career. Combining life with a job is always a difficult balancing act and I think I managed it reasonably well from the point of view of your father and you, but Max would have preferred a stay-at-home mother and has never made any bones about it. I myself would have been miserable without a job, to which my family tradition and education both impelled me, but I have never been an ardent feminist. I respect the dedication of the Lady Thatchers and Kate Adies of this world, but I am much too fond of leisure to have ever considered being an all-out career woman. I like to spend a lot of time at home and am good at domesticity and, above all, I like to potter, which is why I prefer almost any European city to that temple of non-pottering, New York.

After you were born, I made a few rules of life to preserve the balance of work and family and I always stuck to them. I never travelled in the school holidays. I never went to business parties. I kept my weekends free, spending most of them at dear Rose Cottage – Max came too from his earliest days in a moses basket, as did you yourself six years later. All this was made possible, as you know, by Nannie, who stayed with us continuously from six weeks after Max was born until long after we needed a nanny at all. The pay-off to the system of the old-fashioned nanny is that they do in time dominate the house to an absurd degree, and I can fully understand that you, who work harder than I ever did, prefer to employ young, untrained nannies who usually stay for a year and do not get dug in. But some of these are better than others, the annual changes are upsetting, especially if a child and nanny have grown fond of each other, and I don't think I could have tolerated the insecurity of the occasional flighty girl who might bring dubious young men into the house or announce that she is off ski-ing just when you have a burst of extra work. But yours is, I know, the preferred modern choice.

As you partly know, but you were young at the time, my relations with your father worsened as it became increasingly clear that we had few interests or beliefs in common. For years I fostered the conventional hope that our children would be a sufficient bond, but in this I was disappointed. We decided to separate and were divorced in 1962, and your father married Michael Joseph's widow, Anthea, with whom he was extremely happy. Max moved with his father to Anthea's house in the country and you stayed with me in our London flat, with weekends at the cottage, until 1967, when I married Osbert, who had been a widower for several years. I had known Osbert – everyone knew Osbert – for most of my professional life, a figure to chat to at parties, but I did not particularly like him. I thought him supercilious. I saw a little more of him when Mac was editing the *Strand*, and commissioned Osbert to do some caricatures of celebrities, of which the brilliant drawing of Evelyn Waugh has been reproduced all over the world. I still thought him supercilious.

After we separated and Mac had remarried I lived with you fancy-free for some time and was not at all lonely. The relief of being free after an incompatible marriage makes up for the doubtful joys of having a man about the house. I did not have to worry about Mac as he was happy with Anthea, and I was in a job I loved. Then one evening I went to a disheartening cocktail party given by Arthur Christiansen, the most famous of the ex-editors of the *Daily Express*, where I knew not a soul except Osbert, who knew not a soul except me. He suggested that we slide out and have dinner together, which we did, at the only restaurant he knew, the Ritz Grill. From then on we saw more of each other and eventually married, three years after his first wife died in 1964. When a reporter telephoned him to ask, 'Is it true that you and Anne Scott-James are getting married?' he answered, 'Yes, quite true, but you can say that we are still good friends.'

As you know, you and I then moved to Osbert's flat in Eaton Square, which was quite a squeeze, and we all three went to Rose Cottage for most weekends until you were old enough to hive off sometimes with your school-friends. Luckily, you and Osbert clicked from the start, and he loved your company. Our marriage gave me twenty years of happiness, ending only with Osbert's death in 1986, and even now I can scarcely believe my good fortune at meeting and being loved by such a man in my middle age.

By the time I married Osbert I had for long been the last survivor of my own family, which had unfortunately been cursed by ill-health. Daddy and I were the strong ones, both tall and thin, with natural stamina, and Daddy did not die until 1959, at the age of eighty. Mother died at fifty-nine from cancer, but she had never been really well, suffering much from nerves and what were then called 'sick headaches', possibly migraine. My sister Marie had struggled with poor health all her life, and died at the age of fifty. John died at forty after an ill-starred life in which he somehow manage to extract some pleasure from the few small crumbs of opportunity on his plate.

If you sometimes think I am bossy, though you never say so (anyway, I deny it, just 'helpful' is the way I put it), perhaps this potted family history will explain why. If anything practical had to be done, there was just Anne to do it.

Above and right: *When textile impresario Zika Ascher launched a competition for young designers in 1946 he co-opted an expert panel of judges:* left to right *Audrey Withers, editor of* Vogue, *the author, editor of* Harper's Bazaar, *Graham Sutherland (half hidden), Lesley Blanch and Henry Moore.*

On safari in Kenya in 1960, to write a series on wildlife for the Daily Mail. *Masai nomads in the foreground.*

The author's first gardening series appeared in Queen *magazine in 1968. The picture was taken at Rose Cottage.*

Joint ventures with husband Osbert Lancaster: in the garden at Rose Cottage and launching The Pleasure Garden

Osbert

Osbert gave me a new-found sense of security. I don't mean just financial security, though this was pleasant enough after a lifetime of juggling with the bills. The emotional security was the revelation. Osbert was born with a self-confidence rare in my generation. I personally attribute this to his innate talent – there was so much that he did well – but he put it down to the fact that, being five years older than I, he was born into a securer world. He remembered carriages, butlers, bootboys, visiting cards and coming down to tea in a blue silk suit with a Brussels lace collar. I was born when things were already rocky for the middle class, and I cannot remember a time when we were not hard up. Even at school, which he hated – he was at Charterhouse – Osbert coolly disdained the dominant athletic ethos. Standing one afternoon on the football field doing absolutely nothing, he asked a fleet-footed forward, 'Do you wish to pass me on the left or on the right?'

At Oxford he entered as a matter of course the famous charmed circle of the twenties and his friends were John Betjeman, Peter Fleming, Harold Acton, Robert Byron and the rest. He was undismayed when he took a fourth in English, having refused to waste his time on learning Anglo-Saxon but devoting himself to the subjects of his own choice, drawing, writing, acting and architecture. Not for him the sleepless nights spent by so many during the run-up to finals. His professional career as author and artist was fruitful from the start, his first book, *Progress at Pelvis Bay*, being published when he was twenty-eight, soon followed by *Pillar to Post* and *Homes, Sweet Homes*, and the Maudie Littlehampton pocket cartoons in the *Daily Express* started before the war and ran for forty years. Osbert knew what he wanted to do and he did it. He had honourable standards of behaviour and he lived up to them. He was a wise bird, and it was something new in my life to have such support and judgement to rely on.

Living with Osbert was an exhilarating experience, though not the high comedy that foolish people imagined. Nothing maddened me more than when some stranger would say, 'Your life must be a riot of fun, with Maudie in your home and your husband making all those brilliant jokes', as though we rocked with laughter at the breakfast table. True, it was a riot of sorts, but not always of fun. It was a life crowded with happenings and emotions, for at Eaton Square we lived at a social pace such as I had never before experienced, while on the other hand his passion for the arts involved him in many public duties and sometimes battles. No trouble was too much for him to take on behalf of writers and artists or the preservation of good architecture, or the channelling of new building into directions which took account of the human scale. In a single day, he would write a thousand words of a book, go to Fleet Street to draw his cartoon for the *Express*, attend a committee meeting of, say, the Royal Literary Fund or the Royal College of Art, and judge a competition of paintings by handicapped children, talking to them seriously and without a hint of patronage about their work.

Osbert was totally gregarious, which I was not. He hated to be alone, I need a ration of solitude. But our social life dovetailed pretty well because he had a large number of all-male engagements. I loved going with him to dinner parties, for which he was much in demand for his exuberant flow of wit. At one dinner party a very innocent lady said of Guy Burgess, whose disappearance was in the news, 'Some people say he's queer.' '*Queer*', said Osbert, 'you might as well say Paul Robeson had a touch of the tarbrush.' Grand receptions were less easy for me, for Osbert would shamelessly abandon me to fend for myself while he fell into the arms of all the prettiest ambassadresses, whom he had known when he was attached to the Foreign Office for two years after the war. To me, the Foreign Office was *terra incognita*. Another type of engagement which he never missed was a memorial service, which men treat as an enjoyable run-up to a club lunch. Sometimes he was asked to give the address, and he would make the congregation laugh rather than weep, which was much more consoling to the bereaved. Perhaps his happiest times of all were spent designing for the stage, for the whole hubbub of the theatre fulfilled his need for congenial company.

His liking for purely masculine occasions was a mystery to me. I understood, and was slightly jealous of, the club life which claimed him for luncheon nearly every day, for the gossip circulating at the Garrick, the Beefsteak and others was good inside stuff, fodder for the pocket cartoons, and his political dining-clubs sounded delightful. But I marvelled that he enjoyed his numerous City dinners, at which he was often the after-dinner speaker. Nearly every week he would dress up at least once in tails, white tie and the other absurd accessories which fasten with an unaesthetic network of straps and buckles, to attend a function with rich, conventional people. One of his regular dinners was with the Carpenters Company, of which he was a member, rising to be Master for one year – it must have been his strong sense of tradition which involved him, for his forebears had been Carpenters, and he was gratified by the honour of the Mastership. Once a year I had to put on my dowdiest evening dress and attend a Ladies' Night under protest, but usually when he dined in the City I would be asleep when he arrived home, to be woken by the aroma of port which would reach me from the staircase in advance of his own slightly rolling entrance at the bedroom door.

He liked putting on full evening dress, and indeed was known as a dressy man, with cupboards full of expensive clothes including elastic-sided boots and a range of tophats. His usual daytime costume was a suit in a checked pattern, with a pink shirt and a bow tie, 'like an upmarket bookmaker' somebody said, probably himself. He did not usually dress until noon, then he would sail off to a club for lunch, but he had always worked for two hours before this, writing at his large antique desk wearing one of his collection of oriental robes picked up in foreign souks. Even earlier, he had done some creative thinking in the bath, planning his day's ration of one thousand words before sitting at his desk to write them down in his beautiful hand. Osbert's work was a pleasure to him, rarely a struggle.

My happiest times with him were spent travelling, when I had him to myself, but our journeys were so many and so various that I will write about them later.

I do not wish to make our marriage sound like an idyll. Osbert would often say, 'I do not know why I love you so much, you are so absolutely awful', and we would collapse with laughter. For me, the small fly in the ointment of love and security was that Osbert had decided when very young to be helpless in all practical matters, and he could be catastrophically inefficient. In a childhood which was financially prosperous, and with a mother who lavished double affection on him, since she was widowed in the First War and he was an only child, Osbert was spoiled for co-operating in the mechanics of modern living. He behaved during our marriage as though we had a full Edwardian staff from butler to boots. I remember him saying at a dinner party in Eaton Square, 'A little more, my man', giving a gracious smile to an ambassador who was helping me out by going round with the claret. I expected to run the household smoothly and provide lots of good food, which I did, but I had no wish to pick up Osbert's clothes off the floor, pack for him, or make all the travel arrangements, though I soon learned that if I did not undertake the bookings we would land at the wrong airport, when finding a hotel and emergency transport to the desired goal would fall to my lot.

Osbert's attitude to life's chores was candidly confessed in his memoirs. 'For sheer pleasure few methods of progression ... can compare with the perambulator. The motion is agreeable, the range of vision extensive and one has always before one's eyes the rewarding spectacle of a grown-up maintaining prolonged physical exertion ... The gondola, alone, I think, can compare with the pram for pleasure.' One might add, 'or sitting in the passenger seat admiring the scenery while one's wife drives a hired car up a precipitous mountain road at dusk'.

An Invitation from John B.

'I'm giving a lunch party next Tuesday on Southend Pier. Do come – such a lovely ride, just an hour each way by train from Fenchurch Street. Southend is at its best in January, all that icy wind and huge grey waves.'

There was only one person in the world from whom such an invitation would not have received a firm refusal, and that was John Betjeman, always known to his friends as John B. to distinguish him from other Johns, especially John Piper. There was such repressed excitement in John's voice, such a persuasive way of turning all received wisdom on its head, so that Southend in winter sounded more charming than Crete in June, that we accepted with enthusiasm, and, needless to say, the outing was a memorable success. The other guest was John's attractive secretary.

I admit that as we waited for the others in the Fenchurch Street refreshment room my spirits flagged, but once aboard the train, when the quiet voice with the hidden laughter got going, they soared again. John's vast topographical knowledge included the mysteries of the bleak area where east London becomes Essex.

'Keep your eyes open for a really splendid cemetery on the left – it must be the largest in Britain, all overgrown like a jungle. Now move over to the right for Upminster Windmill – oh what a pity it's cloaked in fog. Now back to the left for Basildon New Town; you mustn't miss it at any price, it's the most hideous thing in Britain, an education in itself. Now there's ten miles of absolutely unspoilt country – oh dear, they do seem to have run up a few things, in fact I see it's continuous building all the way. Never mind, we'll soon be at Westcliff, that's the *better* end of Southend. There are some fine 1890 boarding-houses you'll see as we pull out.'

At Southend we travelled to the end of the one-and-a-quarter-mile pier on the miniature railway, had lunch in the restaurant with an expensive claret which we warmed up on the radiator, and walked back to the mainland through one of the most piercing gales I have ever experienced. My plea for a return journey on the miniature railway was turned down. The waves lashed the pier alarmingly.

Then we bought cockles and prawns ('we must buy prawns as a memento of Southend – oh I see they're Norwegian'), looked at an art gallery and a church which seemed to be devoid of any architectural interest whatsoever, and took the train home. It had been a glorious day.

Indeed, in my experience, all days were glorious with John B. I had known him, though not specially well, for many years, and he had contributed to *Harper's Bazaar*.

Later, I came to know John better. Osbert and John had been almost inseparable friends since their Oxford days in the twenties. Their humour, their love of architecture, their deep knowledge of all the arts except music, their phenomenal visual memories, their capacity for enjoyment at every level, their shared religion (high C. of E.), their beautiful voices, their charm, their selfishness, made them two characters who had been cast in the same mould, but hand-finished differently. They both looked extraordinary, John with his rabbity teeth, Osbert with his huge head on a short body and his bulging, all-seeing blue eyes. They were both scintillatingly but effortlessly witty, surpassing themselves in each other's company. Some of my happiest days were spent with the two of them together, staying in John's cottage in Cornwall, or dining in London, or making a quick sortie to see some new exhibition or scandalous building development. John drove us one morning on a tour of the city of London to demonstrate the vandalism round St Paul's, where every one of the old vistas of the cathedral is blocked by rectangular skyscrapers. As John often took his eyes off the road and his hands off the wheel in his excitement, and veered from side to side to catch the right view, it says much for London's drivers that we came out alive. I was more than ready for our strengthening lunch at a fish restaurant where John had thoughtfully booked a table – he was a surprisingly good organization man.

One coincidence in later years almost suggests telepathy between John and Osbert. Osbert and I were staying in Madrid and drove out one cold spring morning to see the Escorial, the forbidding monastery-palace built by the gloomy monarch Philip II, who ended his years there in a cell. A bone-chilling wind was blowing off the barren sierra. As we rounded a corner of the building, clutching our hats and huddling into our overcoats, three people came straight at us on collision course – John and two friends. None of us had any idea that the others were in Spain, let alone at the Escorial. It was uncanny.

Luckily for me, the Escorial was so unprepossessing that neither Osbert nor John wanted to linger. Usually they were indefatigable sightseers. There was no niche nor buttress of a cathedral that they were willing to pass by, no thumbnail sketch in a major exhibition of paintings that they would not pore over. A single parish church would occupy them for two hours, when perhaps we had three or four to see, and I confess that I often grew tired (I am tall and thin, and they were short and stocky), and would rest on a tombstone wondering prosaically when and where we would lunch. This poor-spirited response would not attack me often, and only when my back, my feet and my brain gave way together, because both Osbert and John were incomparable guides.

I think John was at his happiest in Cornwall. He loved the breezy walks along the sea-shore with the sea-birds mewing, and his warm, comfortable cottage with an apple-orchard and a stream in the garden. Though not addicted to 'kiddies' in close proximity, he enjoyed the nostalgia of the bucket-and-spade activity on the sands, which reminded him of his own childhood. He liked the high seas in winter and the Atlantic gales – he was never a man for the Mediterranean – and the Cornish legends and customs. A day in John's cottage would go something like this. After breakfast John indulges a horrid habit of reading aloud from an old book of Cornish jokes, and in spite of protests that bad jokes could not be borne so early in the day he grinds remorselessly on.

'I don't think any of you know this one, it is really first class.

'"Bob: 'They say Simpson gave you a black eye.'

'"Dick: 'That just shows how people exaggerate. I had the eye already, he merely laid on the colour.'"'

We all think this quite funny, but when our host starts again, 'There's a good yarn going round about a motorist', we remove the joke book by force.

In the mornings we usually walk along the beach or the cliffs, John and Osbert, the two Old Tops, often stopping in spite of the Atlantic gale to plunge into an orgy of discussion, pivoting about on their heels and brandishing their walking-sticks in their excitement. 'Come *on*,' the rest of us say, 'it's too cold to hang about.'

In the afternoon we tour in the car, John taking us to his favourite places, but also keen that we should not miss an eyesore. 'There used to be kingfishers here, but they don't like the pylons, which I suppose are more useful, really.' We take a wrong turning and there are recriminations and a short sharp row blows up about the best way home. Each of us is convinced that only he or she knows how to read a map.

Back home, we dine well, drink like fish, and take old books from the shelves and old prints from the walls, and the talk turns antiquarian until John indulges in another joke. He dives into the fish-basket which serves him for a briefcase and extracts a catalogue of 'garden ornaments and reproductions' from which we are all to choose a favourite item. 'I think I'd like this ornate fisherman in an antique finish standing two foot high.' He might finish the evening reading us Tennyson before we go to bed.

John died after much illness two years before Osbert who, in his own last years, was also ill and melancholy, and would often rend my heart by saying 'Oh dear, I do miss John B.'

The Garden Door

I had been married to Osbert for over a year when I turned over in my mind the idea of becoming a freelance. I had had a full-time job for more than thirty years and the idea of having more freedom had a certain appeal. 'What shall I do this morning?' would be a novel waking thought. Osbert was willing and able to support me. But I had fears, a mild fear that I would be lost without the framework to life which a job provides, a stronger fear that I would grow lazy. It is easier to write when a deadline threatens you and your work provokes immediate comment than when you have to generate your own energy, and I had no wish to give up writing and turn into a cabbage. If I gave up my personal column on the *Daily Mail*, to which I was much attached, I would have to find another subject to make my own.

Poised on the brink, my decision to jump was settled by the new young editor of *Queen* Magazine, Hugh Johnson. I was on holiday with Osbert in France in the spring of 1968 when I received a telegram from Hugh asking me to take on a series of articles on gardening, and I accepted by return. I had been a devoted gardener all my life, and an occasional gardening writer, but was neither a botanist nor a trained horticulturalist, and I had everything to learn. As soon as we were back in England, I bought some reference books, set off on a study tour of English gardens, and consulted as many specialists as I could. Hugh was in a hurry to get started.

I abandoned any idea of writing how-to-do-it articles, because I was not qualified to be didactic and anyway that is not my style. I would try to see gardens through the eyes of the gifted people who had created them. I wanted to choose gardens which would be individual or even eccentric, exciting in design or plantsmanship or both, and probably not very large, so that the reader could glean ideas rather admire from afar. I began with a feature about John Piper, whose farmhouse garden was a masterpiece of art concealing art, with patches of colour which owed much to his painter's eye and homely touches, such as chives among the roses, and vegetables in the borders, which derived from his love of kitchens, food, domesticity and craftsmanship. I progressed to Rhoda Birley, widow of the painter Sir Oswald Birley, whose Sussex manor-house garden was supremely romantic, made so by hundreds of climbing plants weaving or scrambling to the sky, roses, clematis, honeysuckles, wisteria, making mysterious draperies over walls and trees. I went later to visit Mrs Margery Fish in Somerset, a plantswoman and plant collector without equal. Herself a gardening writer with a national following, she gave me one piece of advice which I have never forgotten. 'Write about your mistakes', she said. 'That's what people want to hear about. If you, too, have put a clematis in too hot a place, and confess it, your readers feel that you are not a lecturer, but a friend.' Her plants were her friends, too, and she thought of them as people, needing affection as well as food and drink.

After two years I felt brave enough to write my first gardening book, bearing Mrs Fish's philosophy in mind, and since then have written nine more, ranging from a history of British gardening, which Osbert illustrated with marvellously witty drawings encapsulating each period, to an essay on flowers in ancient art for the British Museum. The best-known is *Sissinghurst: the Making of a Garden*. My publisher, Michael Joseph, had been the publisher of Vita Sackville-West's gardening books, and early in 1973 Anthea Joseph and Nigel Nicolson invited me to write the story of the creation of that glorious garden by Nigel's parents, Harold Nicolson and Vita Sackville-West. This was a plum assignment which was to take me shuttling to and from Sissinghurst for the best part of a year.

The book was published in 1975, was a best-seller for several weeks, and became a sort of passport into the inner circles of the gardening world. This is very much of a club of which all the members, wherever they live, seem to know each other. Plantsmen, designers, head gardeners, nurserymen, were among my new friends, and I visited many of their gardens, even travelling by invitation as far as Georgia, USA. I worked particularly hard to learn more about plants, a subject so vast that I am often depressed at how much I do not and will never know.

In 1978 I received a totally unexpected invitation to be a member of Council of that august body, the Royal Horticultural Society. I cannot pretend that this honour was wholly due to my gardening expertise. The less flattering truth was that the RHS was trying to improve its anti-feminist image and needed a statutory woman for the all-male Council. (I had done two stints some years earlier on the Council of the Royal College of Art for the same reason, though admittedly I knew much more about art than horticulture). There had been only one woman before me, Frances Perry, a brilliant professional gardener, and a hard act to follow.

Of course I accepted with alacrity and sat on Council for four exhilarating years with the added privilege of sitting on one of the RHS judging committees. As you know, I still judge plants at most of the RHS fortnightly shows, and have a field day at the Chelsea Flower Show. 'Staging faultless ... a thin vase at the back ... peak condition ... dirty pots ... roses haven't taken up the water ... healthy foliage', I mutter, and other judges' abracadabra.

Working at Sissinghurst

To write a book about the garden at Sissinghurst was an exhilarating project, but also a daunting one. The responsibility of making such an important record was great. Nigel, like his parents, was a distinguished writer and a publisher and was likely to be critical. There were hundreds of plants in the garden which I did not know. The head gardeners were all-powerful and might not like me. I soon learned that I was not the first, but the third writer who had embarked on the task, the other two having fallen by the wayside within days of starting, and I had no wish to suffer the same ignominious fate.

The sources of material were rich. Nigel himself was right behind me from start to finish, with clear memories not only of Sissinghurst as far back as 1930, when the Nicolsons bought it, the garden a dump of old bedsteads and sardine tins matted with weeds, but also of the first garden made by Harold and Vita at Long Barn, near Sevenoaks, which was a sort of trial run for Sissinghurst. (Nigel took me took me to see Long Barn on my first visit.) The written records were unusually abundant, consisting of Nicolson letters, diaries, plant lists and planting plans, all kept in Nigel's house at Sissinghurst and meticulously catalogued by Nigel himself. The joint head gardeners, Pamela Schwerdt and Sybille Kreutzberger, were infinitely skilled and knowledgeable, and had worked for Vita for three years before her death. For self-revelation of the personalities of the two who created the garden, there were Harold's prodigious diaries and Vita's books. There were also photographs of the garden at various stages.

Luckily, Nigel's *Portrait of a Marriage*, though completed when I began my work, was not published until the autumn of 1973, so that I had formed my own impression of Vita before I read it, and Victoria Glendinning's brilliant but cruel biography, *Vita*, came out much later. A combination of these and other books made Vita seem something of a monster, and she was undeniably an egotist, but, working for many hours in the garden and among the letters and books, I came to like her very much. Sissinghurst scandals were not, thank God, part of my brief.

Nigel lives in the main house by the front courtyard at

Sissinghurst, which had been Vita's quarters in her lifetime, Harold having a separate cottage, while the boys' bedrooms and the dining-room were in yet another building, the old Priest's House. Vita also had a charming sitting-room in the Elizabethan tower, which was preserved after her death as she had arranged it, with little jugs of flowers on her desk, a portrait of the Brontë sisters on the wall, a photograph of Harold, a shelf of favourite gardening books and a mass of her own notebooks. When I went to Sissinghurst, I usually stayed for a night and I slept in Vita's own room, with windows overlooking the garden on two sides.

To me, Vita had a physical presence in that house, in the tower, in every corner of the garden. The letters and notes I read were original, in her handwriting, and anything a hand has touched leaves traces of personality. In the white garden I experienced a little of Vita's elation when she first saw in her mind's eye a sea of grey foliage pierced by tall white flowers and hoped that 'the grey ghostly barn-owl will sweep silently across a pale garden next summer in the twilight'. In the rose garden, I was infected by her romantic love of profusion, her desire to 'cram, cram, cram every chink and cranny'.

The atmosphere at Sissinghurst was so intense that sometimes I felt that I was staying in a religious precinct. The house was very old. I was living among Vita's relics. In the evenings I would dine with Nigel if he was at home, and we would talk about his family and the history of the garden. The head gardeners were fanatically dedicated and worked seemingly night and day to make the planting more beautiful every year. Neighbours and tenants were eager with reminiscences of the Nicolsons. There were souvenirs and memories everywhere – a plaque of three Greek bishops brought home by the Nicolsons from Constantinople, bronze urns from the château of Bagatelle, a present from Vita's mother. The very plants were objects of reverence, like the great rondel of yew which Harold had put in as little plants in 1932. Sometimes I found it all overcharged with personal history and would flee to the village inn for a drink.

Ten years later I wrote a book about the garden at Glyndebourne in collaboration with Christopher Lloyd, which was just as enjoyable, but in a different way. Again, the house is old, the garden lovely, and the family tradition strong, for Sir George Christie, who lives there, and so magnificently maintains the opera, is the son of John Christie, who founded Glyndebourne Opera in the 1930s. But the Christies live as much in the present and future as in the past, and there are few early records of the garden, so that I felt no uneasy twinges of nostalgia, no ghostly hauntings.

I worked intermittently on *Sissinghurst* for a year, for I wanted to see the garden at every season, and then went down with my manuscript to Sissinghurst feeling nervous and low. First I spent an evening going through it with Pam and Sybille, and I am afraid I had made many mistakes as to the plants. These they patiently corrected. Throughout the year they had been generous with their time and indulgent with my ignorance. Next day I worked on the corrections and gave Nigel the manuscript in the evening, expecting to hear from him in a week or so, which I would spend in apprehension, as though waiting for exam results. But he read the book overnight and in the morning told me that he liked it. I was overwhelmed with relief.

Since then there have been many books about Sissinghurst and about Vita herself, of which *Portrait of a Marriage* created an international sensation and was later adapted for a television series which I can only describe as steamy. When I worked at Sissinghurst, which is a small garden, the number of visitors had already become a problem, but it could still be seen at off-peak times in comfort. Now, after an excess of publicity, it has become a prime tourist attraction, with queues, shops and multiple facilities, a far cry from the quiet paradise where from 1938 on Vita sometimes sat at a table proudly collecting coins in a bowl from occasional visitors whom she called 'the shillingses'. She enjoyed their interest and would answer their gardening questions, unlike Harold, who disliked them.

My days at Sissinghurst, though in some ways alarming, gave me deep pleasure and intensified my love of plants, and because Sissinghurst is an intimate garden, not majestic or grand, I found there was much I could learn there to help me with my own amateurish plot.

A Whirl Round France

Working as a freelance required certain adjustments in both my attitude to journalism and my literary style. Freelancing is an independent life and you have to be your own taskmaster, working to a self-imposed discipline, or you would sit back and do nothing at all. Luckily, I had been so long in Fleet Street that I had many editorial friends to egg me on, including the charming and much-lamented Charles Douglas-Home, then editor of *The Times*, who commissioned some features, and the doyenne of film critics, Dilys Powell, who had already wangled me on to the radio programme *My Word!*, on which I spent joyous evenings over many years working with Dilys and the sparkling Denis Norden and Frank Muir. I think that for a young journalist without contacts freelancing must be an anxious way of life, especially today, when the golden days of Fleet Street are in the past and proprietors are hungry for vanishing profits. Also you have to accept that, writing for many outlets, you are not going to be loved, either by your employers or your readers, as much as a regular contributor with a personal following. At first I missed the popularity, but the compensations of leisure and relief from pressure soon outweighed the loss.

On the technical side I was puzzled that so many commissioning editors asked me for articles 'in-depth', for it was not a phrase used on the *Express* or the *Mail*, or even on the serious-minded *Picture Post*. However, I soon found that 'in-depth' really meant 'at-length', and I had to elongate my normally pithy style to fill articles of at least two thousand words and often much more. The *Sunday Times* was particularly keen on 'in-depth' pieces and I strove to achieve the required profundity. I wrote a long feature for the *Sunday Times* in 1968 about the life of the current generation of girls at Oxford for which I spent a week as the guest of my old college, Somerville. I scandalized some readers by reporting, among more important matters, that many of the female undergraduates lived in digs with their boyfriends, and one outraged father telephoned the Somerville authorities to say that if this appalling report were

true he would withdraw his daughter at once. It is hard to believe that this happened less than twenty-five years ago.

The freelance assignment which I remember most vividly was a joint undertaking with Osbert and Patrick Lichfield. We had been commissioned by Hugh Johnson to fill a whole special number of *Queen* with a feature on France, Patrick contributing the photographs, Osbert the drawings, and I the words, for which I prepared myself by reading Henry James's delightful *A Little Tour in France*.

Hugh is a journalist rich in brave ideas and now an internationally famed expert on wine, but at that time, when he was very young, his grand strategies were better than his attention to detail. Our tour which he designed to cover almost every region of France in two weeks – Normandy, the Loire, the Dordogne, the Gorges du Tarn, the Camargue and Provence on the way out, and back by Burgundy and the Pas de Calais – ran into difficulties from Day One.

We were to travel in a chauffeur-driven Rolls-Royce, flying with the car from Lydd in Kent to Calais, and Hugh came to see us all off at Eaton Square. There were five of us on the trip including the chauffeur and Patrick's American assistant, Billy, plus our luggage, Patrick's luggage, and a mountain of camera equipment, and we were not a little put out when the hearse-sized car we had expected turned out to be the latest Rolls-Royce sports coupé. That was the first hurdle. Patrick surmounted it by sending Billy by taxi to fetch his photographic van, with instructions to follow us at top speed to Lydd in the forlorn hope of catching our plane, or, if he missed it, to take the next one. Then off went Patrick, Osbert and I crammed like sardines in our Rolls, leaving Hugh on the telephone trying to book a place for the second vehicle. By exerting charm at Lydd and holding up the plane, we managed to get both cars on board, if you could call the van a car. Its maximum speed was fifty miles an hour, and we had to put in long hours of driving to keep up with our schedule.

But even this was too much for the Rolls-Royce. It broke down at regular intervals, with a final collapse on our last day at Arras, where half the population of the town crowded joyfully round to exclaim at '*cette jolie voiture Anglaise qui ne marche pas*'. Every Frenchman present seemed to be an amateur mechanic, and helpful suggestions were not lacking. Our humiliation was profound.

The Rolls in tandem with the van was not the only difficulty. The month was March, the season backward, the weather grey, and even in the south poor Patrick had a struggle to record one smiling, leafy landscape. It was easier for Osbert, sketching in black-and-white, choosing any subject he fancied from a fish-market to a château, and for me, with a writer's licence to imagine what I could not see.

Another problem was that the Rolls and the van tended to get separated. The former carried the chauffeur, Osbert and myself, while Patrick and Billy rode in the van, and our interests were not always identical. I, who was unwillingly thrust into the post of leader responsible for the party, wanted to record as many aspects of French life as possible. Osbert wanted architecture, and Patrick looked for scenery with time off for gastronomy. It is to our credit that the only cross words exchanged in two weeks occurred when I insisted on lunching at a *relais routier*, to sample run-of-the-mill French cooking, though there was a two-rosette restaurant only three miles away. I suggested that Patrick and Billy make for the restaurant while Osbert and I gathered local colour in the *relais*, but was disgusted to see Osbert climbing into Patrick's van, leaving me to lunch alone with the lorry drivers.

Later, we formed the habit of splitting into two parties by day, each gathering our own journalistic material, with arrangements to meet at our chosen hotel in the evening for a champagne dinner. As the hotels booked for us by *Queen* were often two hundred miles apart or more, our working time was alarmingly short. Never have I collected impressions and notes so fast, never has Osbert sketched at such speed, but he was never put out by difficult conditions, or bothered by admiring crowds jogging his pen. On one occasion a kind policeman held his mackintosh cape over Osbert's head to keep off the rain.

The night which was to be the high-spot of our tour was at the celebrated Beaumanière hotel at Les Baux, in Provence (five spoons-and-forks and three rosettes in Michelin), and we were just sitting down to dinner and sipping the first of many wines when we heard a cheery voice saying, 'Oh there you are, you lucky beggars', to find that Hugh Johnson had flown out with his beautiful wife Judy for a night to see how we were getting on. He was surprised at the coolness of his reception. 'You should have joined us at that awful fake ranch you booked for us in the Camargue where they served horsemeat steaks and chips', I said crisply, but by the fifth exquisite course we had forgiven him.

In the end the feature was accomplished and filled some twenty pages of the magazine. Though not best pleased when friends said, 'What a marvellous time you must have had', we forgot the ordeals we had been through to create our *reportage* on France and remembered only the good times. As you know, I have worked with many celebrated photographers in my life, among them Cecil Beaton, Dahl-Wolfe, Bert Hardy, Richard Avedon, Tony Snowdon, Cartier-Bresson, Bill Brandt, but I have never known one more good-humoured than Patrick. The three of us returned home not only on speaking terms, but friends for life, and sometimes I feel quite a twinge of envy when I ask you, dear Clare, what you are going to do tomorrow and you say, 'I'm working with Patrick Lichfield.'

Travels with Osbert

One of the blessings for which I thank my stars is that I travelled to so many memorable places before they were swamped by mass tourism. Not only before the war, but as lately as thirty years ago, which was roughly the date of the coach explosion, you could meander by car or bus through Provence, the Dordogne, Wales, Perthshire, Apulia, Sicily, Yugoslavia, Turkey, and stop when the spirit moved you in the certainty of finding a bed for the night and a simple meal. There was always plenty of space to park a car, if you had one,, just outside the church or château you wanted to see, you could wander at will among the massive pillars of Stonehenge or stroll through the sacred shrines of Delphi as the stars came out. The sense of freedom was at its most beguiling in the wilds of Greece. The mountain roads were empty, every bay on the Aegean invited you to scramble down the rocks for a secluded swim, only the most famous classical sites were heavily frequented, and the Byzantine churches attracted no interest at all. I had travelled as much as I could, having little time or money, before the war, but my happiest excursions were more leisurely and penetrating and took place between twenty and thirty years ago when I travelled with Osbert, which was a rich experience in itself.

On the plus side was Osbert's profound knowledge of architecture and his enthusiasm for local life, especially in Greece. How could you fail to absorb a little of the Byzantine system with a companion who would gaze for a long time in

wonder at the perfect balance of a dome? On the minus side (and I paid the small price gladly) was that I was not only his travelling companion, but his chauffeur, courier, caterer, porter, accountant, cash-provider, telephonist and interpreter, even in countries where he knew the language much better than I did. I had been twice to Greece before I met Osbert, but he had actually lived in Athens in the Embassy for two years from 1944, when he was attached to the Foreign Office. Yet it was I who trekked down the mountain with a phrasebook to find a plumber when the lavatory overflowed at the ravishing but ramshackle farmhouse we had taken one August in the Peloponnese. Osbert remained drinking ouzo on the terrace sketching the pine-tree in whose shade he sat, calmly awaiting the man with the plunger. I must add that I was richly rewarded for being the errand-girl, for Osbert gave me his sketch, which was very beautiful and is one of my best-loved possessions.

We both loved Greece above all other countries. Osbert had been both enraptured and amused during the happy days of his Greek posting; I was partly influenced by a classical education, partly spellbound by the amber light, the herb-scented mountains, the ubiquitous traces of the old civilization – sometimes a broken column or two in the middle of an unfrequented valley would revive the past more vividly than the famous restored and signposted sites. Before my travels with Osbert I had thought only about classical Greece, but when we married, Osbert had already collected some sketches of Byzantine churches for a book he had in mind, later published as *Sailing to Byzantium*. Together we searched out many more, both famous and obscure, in Turkey, Yugoslavia, Italy, even France, but mostly in Greece and the Greek islands. Here again, it was often the smaller churches which moved me most. As Osbert himself wrote:

> They are infinitely far removed from the pomp and glitter of S. Vitale or Hagia Sophia. Nevertheless at high noon, when the silence is broken only by the buzzing of the wild bees which have nested on top of the iconostasis, and the air is heavy with the smell of honey-wax candles and the wild thyme on the threshold, it is in such humble shrines as these that one may, perhaps, come closest to understanding the message of Orthodoxy.

Though we sometimes went abroad to stay with friends, most

often with Alan and Lucy Moorehead in their joyously hospitable villa in Italy, Osbert was a dedicated worker, and I think we spent more time in aggregate travelling with a purpose, that being collection of material for a book. Then we travelled light, with no smart clothes, and Osbert did not clamour for luxury, indeed he loathed large hotels. Our journeys often involved patient detective work, for some of the churches we wanted to find, though beautiful in architecture and decoration, were small and obscure, and the guidebooks of thirty years ago were often hopelessly inaccurate. This was particularly true of Kastoria, in northern Greece, which is now a stopping-place for many a coach tour, but it applied to minor churches even in Istanbul, where the less important old buildings were often swallowed up in slums. But we would hang on like terriers, trace and retrace our steps ask and ask again, until we found our goal, perhaps a church listed in a learned book of the last century. When working, Osbert had no thoughts about comfort and we often stopped for the night in cottages which were quite rugged, with lumpy beds and Turkish-style lavatories far off among the chickens. Osbert preferred a picnic to a taverna lunch, and I became accomplished at making good picnics with melons, ham, bread, olives, goat's cheese and wine, with cutlery and napkins which I had bought in Athens, and I never forgot the corkscrew. In those days most cars had removable seats so that one could sit in comfort under a tree on ground baked hard by the sun, and doze off peacefully after lunch.

One special problem in the remoter districts was the shortage of company for Osbert who, indefatigably gregarious, would get bored with just me in the evenings. But sometimes, as we sat at a café after dinner in quite a lonely spot I would hear the welcome cry of, 'Good Lord, there's Osbert', and out of the mountain night there would appear some sophisticated friend. But his best companion was his work, for every day he sketched in his large, cloth-bound sketchbook, and in the early evening would sit at a café table and compose a well-informed and witty commentary on the sights and incidents of our day, writing it into his book in an impeccable hand. (I have six of these annotated sketchbooks in all and often look through them with melancholy delight.) If a book was going well and his drawings were up to his exacting standard, the lack of company did not bother him.

On a long drive, Osbert would sometimes take a turn at the wheel, for which I would be grateful at first, but so frightful was his driving, for he was too lazy to change gear, preferring to stall the car going up a mountain or to rely on the brakes going down, that I preferred to do most of the job myself. Once, on our way to Kastoria, I somehow managed to miss the road and we found ourselves on a narrow stony track with a hairpin bend every few hundred yards which led presumably to some mountain village. All such roads, I knew from experience, had a bus along them twice a day, and there was no possible place to turn, just the mountain on one side and a precipice on the other. I had decided what to do if we met the bus and rehearsed some suitable phrases and explanatory gestures. I would take our suitcases out of the boot, hand the bus-driver the keys and indicate to him that he could do what he liked with the car – reverse it, or push it over the precipice if need be, or, better still, reverse the bus, but back the car myself round the hairpin bends I would not do. No bus came, and after a few miles we reached a village where we could turn and zigzag back again, after checking the bus timetable.

While we were pausing and stretching our legs in this desolate spot, a girl came up to us and said in the brittle accent of New York, 'You look lost, can I help you?' We talked, of course, and discovered that the poor child had suffered the fate of many Americans who marry a foreigner without knowing much about his origins. Her husband was Greek and had wanted to take her home to meet his family, who were peasants in this village, and the girl had suffered quite a culture shock. 'I can tell you', she said gloomily, 'that I am not too happy with this place.' We tried to cheer her by pointing out that she would soon be home in dear old New York, and that she was lucky to have such a beautiful destination for holidays, but she would not be comforted. I later met an American girl in the same state of identity confusion in Japan. She had married a Japanese in the United States and returned with her husband to Tokyo, where he expected her to live Japanese fashion as something akin to a slave.

Our Byzantine searches took us in the course of two or three years to many countries, even as far north as the Loire valley, where there is a ninth-century Byzantine church at Germigny-des-Près. Though it is not the most popular of his books, *Sailing to Byzantium* gave me immense personal gratification, for I shared so much of the research. Of all our Byzantine destinations, I loved Mistra most, not only for its wealth of churches, but because we went there directly from Kastoria in northern Greece, which is green and rainy, with scrubby vegetation, and it felt like going home to be back among the olive groves and baked, herb-scented earth of the Peloponnese.

The place where Osbert's intellectual and social needs, and my romantic ones, fused to perfection, was in Crete. But as you, dear child, joined us on one of our Cretan excursions, as on many other occasions where the vivacity of your company *just* outweighed the hazards of having under one's wing a hyperactive teenager bent on pleasure, I will write another letter about travelling with Osbert – and you.

Teenager in Tow

Though parents and toddlers can, I am told, spend their holidays in unruffled harmony, the generation gap often yawns when the once biddable little children reach their teens. I dare say there *are* families in which the parents are crazy about discos or the children's thirst for sightseeing can scarcely be quenched, but they are rare. Usually, interests clash.

In your case, both Osbert and I loved having you in tow on our travels – you were so amusing and intelligent and easy to please – but there were hazards, not least your capacity for getting mislaid.

We nearly lost you in Athens, when you joined us for what proved to be an idyllic holiday in Crete. You must have been thirteen. Before you came out, Osbert and I had been travelling through Crete in our usual pursuit of churches, guided at the western end of the island by Osbert's old friend, the painter John Craxton, who lived in Canea. One day he took us to the village of Platanias, eight miles to the west, for a swim, and it was the most beautiful place in the world. The beach was dotted with sand-lilies and fringed with oleanders and I was seized with a romantic conviction that this was paradise and I must stay there. The only lodging Johnnie could find for us was a cottage, shed, shack, call it what you will, for a few shillings a week. It was whitewashed and nestled in a grove of tamarisk, with the beach at the back and a patch of parched common-land in front grazed by a goat, a mule, a donkey and innumerable hens. A stream babbled past the door, there was a well, a trellis dripping with vines, and a spectacular view of the village, which was carved out of perpendicular cliffs.

Loyally, we left it all and flew back to Athens to collect you at the airport. Your plane taxied in, the passengers streamed across the tarmac, no Clare. As despair and guilt gripped us, you descended last of all in the company of an air hostess. We hurried to the barrier, hugged you and welcomed you, but you seemed disgruntled. What had happened?

'I've had a terrible journey. Daddy saw me off and handed me over to an air hostess, and they made me wear this shaming thing' – you tore off a badge marked 'Unaccompanied Minor' – and then they put me on the wrong plane, it was going to Frankfurt. They discovered just in time and I was rushed across the airport to the Athens plane, which was kept waiting, so the passengers looked at me with hate. But worse followed. There was another Unaccompanied Minor on the plane, a *baby*, and they thought we would be happy together and I had to hold the baby the whole way. They even gave me its bottle, so I couldn't get at my lunch. I will definitely not travel care of the airline again. I say, it's hot, could I have an ice?'

We soothed you and whisked you off to the Grande Bretagne for the night, and then we all left for Crete at dawn the next morning to find our cottage.

How well do you remember it? It lacked all forms of mod. con. and consisted of one room and a kitchen, furnished with a table and chairs and three frightful beds. Hens wandered through it all day and the goat would slip its tether and try its luck in the kitchen, while sand whirled in and out borne on the stiff Cretan breezes. We christened it the Henhouse. It was primitive, but heavens, it was beautiful.

My first task was to take the bus into Canea to buy a few comforts, but when your stay is going to be only a week, you get pretty mean. I bought one sheet apiece, jugs and a bowl, we had

our picnic cutlery, and Johnnie lent us some pillows which, like all Greek pillows, felt like sacks filled with melons.

Platanias was a hive of sociability. Osbert's love of company was gratified by Johnnie, who came over from Canea, our much-travelled friend, Coote Lygon, who was staying near by, and Stephen Spender's son and a friend, who were spending the whole summer in Platanias, and adopted you. The villagers, filled with the same curiosity which sent the Greeks exploring three thousand years ago, came in droves to have a look at us, some filling their pitchers at the well, others calling to check that I had fed the mangy tame pigeon which had been bequeathed as a landlord's fixture. Our landlord had also left a hawk-eyed granny in the village to keep an eye on the property, though there was nothing to steal. More welcome than granny was the sergeant of police, who grew sunflowers and brought me a present of a sunflower every day.

The only serious trouble was the noise. The Greeks are always building houses or knocking them down, and all day the throb of construction or demolition would shatter the air. By night the jukeboxes bellowed their tunes until the arrival of the rosy-fingered, when the braying of donkeys and the crowing of a thousand cocks would take over. The work at the cottage also proved quite taxing, what with drawing water, gathering brushwood and cleaning the sand out of the scrambled eggs, and whenever I urgently needed help I would find that Osbert had gone off with his sketchbook and your dear little head was bobbing up and down two hundred yards out at sea, regardless of my strict ban on solitary bathing, for the calm Cretan sea can grow rough without warning. At the Henhouse I thought I detected a certain amount of ganging up between Osbert and you.

In the end, it was I who crumpled first, Osbert being perfectly happy with the simple life when there were so many friends for conversation and so many scenes to draw, and we closed down the cottage and took a boat to the eastern end of the island to stay in a comfortable new hotel made up of separate cottages. It was on an isolated headland and had a good Egyptian chef, but the hotel is now third-rate and the bare headland has turned into a town.

I must admit, dearest child, that I do seem to associate our threesome holidays with a certain amount of anxiety. In the

Dordogne, you forgot to get off the night train at Brive, where we were lined up on the platform to meet you. In Sardinia, our suitcases arrived off the plane, but yours went on to Karachi. In Corsica, you came with a youth who could neither digest foreign food nor swim. But all too soon for us, you were old enough to take independent holidays with your own friends, and it is a tribute to the charm of your company that when I later travelled alone with Osbert he would often turn to me and exclaim, 'This would be just the place for Clare.'

The Common Lot

It is rare good fortune, darling Clare, if the great days in a human life last to the end. Perhaps it only happens to those who die young. For the rest of us, health gives way or friends or family die, leaving us bereft. Osbert and I were not among the lucky ones.

I had intended to skate over the years from 1975 to 1986, or leave them out, because the things which happened to me were purely personal, of no general interest, but unless I sketch them in lightly it may seem as though I had passed them in exile or in prison, or been otherwise *hors de combat*. I was around, in London, but living quietly.

In 1975 Osbert had his major operation followed by a slight stroke which left his sight impaired, a terrible blow for an artist. For several years, as you know, we managed to keep up many of our old activities, but for Osbert, the enjoyer of all enjoyers, the party was over.

For some weeks after his stroke he could not see to draw, but he gradually adjusted to working with partial eyesight and resumed his cartoons for the *Daily Express*. Then, a more difficult achievement, he illustrated the book which I wrote for the express purpose of getting him back to work, *The Pleasure Garden*, which John Murray published in 1977. I am proud of that book, because Osbert was deeply depressed at the time and needed the encouragement of a serious project. I think his garden drawings are as scholarly and funny as any in his early architectural books, such as *Homes, Sweet Homes*.

For several years after 1975 we were able to travel, going in the first summer to stay with Alan and Lucy Moorehead in Porto Ercole, where Osbert, who dearly loved Lucy, was as happy as he was ever to be. In the next summer we went to Cos, in the next to Corfu, in the next to Crete, and in 1979 to Porto Ercole again, our last major outing. Osbert enjoyed Corfu because the island was full of English friends who entertained and cherished us. The holiday began inauspiciously, because driving from the airport to our modest villa I had the only car accident of my life. It was dusk, the road was atrocious and I was dog tired after a belated flight, and I bounced off a pothole into a stone wall, cracking two ribs myself and giving Osbert a gash in his leg which required stitches. I spent the night in hospital, which was like the Crimea, Osbert in a hotel, but the saintly travel agents (I am a walking advertisement for Corfu Villas) drove us to our villa the next day, reports of our mishap travelled on the Corfu grapevine, and kind friends called, brought provisions and took us out for meals. The kindest friend of all brought me some painkillers. A few days later Jacob Rothschild sent his boat to fetch us for a day at his villa and one of his guests, the eye specialist, Patrick Trevor-Roper, took Osbert's stitches out with a pair of eyebrow tweezers to cheers and clapping from the onlookers. Osbert rather enjoyed this incident and never complained of the pain of his wound, nor reproached me for the accident.

Our Cretan foray was not a success. Osbert was miserable at the development of eastern Crete since our last visit and I was devoured by anxiety at having taken him in declining health so far from home. Our final visit to the Mooreheads in Italy was, as always, a pleasure, but our happiness was overshadowed by Lucy's death in a car accident a few days after we arrived back in London.

It was in 1977 that we moved from Eaton Square (you having left the nest long before), which was a glamorous but inconvenient flat on two floors, with stairs all over the place, to my present flat in Chelsea, less splendid, but all on one floor and easier for an invalid. Personally, I prefer Chelsea to Belgravia any day.

Through those ten years my work ticked over and I did as much as I could to keep my hand in without leaving home for more than a few hours at a time. I wrote a good many articles, mostly on gardening, continued on the radio panel game *My Word!*, which gave me the relaxation of cheerful evenings recording the programmes with true friends, and from 1978 my work for the Royal Horticultural Society was an absorbing interest. Towards the end of Osbert's life, doctors and nurses filled the flat and visits from you or Cara,* who always cheered him immensely, and from a necessarily diminishing band of friends; kept us going until 1986 when Osbert died, here in Chelsea. I have been just half a person ever since.

*Osbert's daughter by his first wife, Karen.

A Worm in the British Museum

Why do I tremble at the knees whenever I enter the British Museum? Is it the ferocity of the Assyrian reliefs with their processions of bloody conquest? Is it the all-pervading Egyptian obsession with death? Is it the sheer size of the building with its echoing galleries and hot, dry atmosphere? No, it is the knowledge that I am an intellectual worm. This sad piece of self-enlightenment was brought home to me when I wrote a book (or strictly, a third of a book) for this august establishment. Generations of lofty scholars have unconsciously conspired to build up the worm-sensation in all outsiders, so that you cringe before keepers, assistant keepers, lecturers and all the authorities who know so very, very much about their subjects, who are soaked in their manuscripts and inscriptions, their hieroglyphs and cuneiform, and who cannot imagine what on earth you are doing in their department trying to write a book about it.

What I was doing there is easily explained. Over the years, I had expanded the length of my writing, first from column paragraphs to newspaper and magazine features and then to books, of which I had published seven by 1987, including *Sissinghurst* and *The Pleasure Garden*, my book with Osbert. In that year the editors of British Museum Publications asked me to write a book about floral decoration on sculpture, ceramics, jewellery and other works of art in the Museum collections, excluding painting, which had already been the subject of a glorious book.

I was at first flattered, but it took a mere two days for me to learn that I was not up to it. I spent these days wandering through the Museum looking for floral patterns and flower-shaped objects in a state of ignorant bewilderment, especially in the Oriental galleries, and I realized that the task would take me ten years of which the first five would have to be spent studying eastern art. So the editors suggested that the book be divided into three parts, and that if I took on the floral art of the Ancient World, they would invite two experts to write the sections on Western Art and Oriental Art, and this was arranged. My only claim to attempting the Ancient World was that I knew a little ancient history and have good Greek and Latin, but I soon discovered that I could have done with some knowledge of Egyptian and Assyrian as well.

So long as you are happy with your worm status, which I was, working in the Museum can be an enormous pleasure. You never doubt that what you are doing is worthwhile, because much of it has not been done before, and are quite proud at the end of the day to have your name on a beautifully produced and meticulously checked BM publication. There are many kind people at the Museum who, once you have convinced them that you are not an imbecile, are willing to help you. The keepers are the best bet, because they seem to have time to spare. They may even unbend so far as to have a cup of coffee with you. You may meet opposition lower down in the scale, where junior scholars have not yet written all the books they want to write and would like to be doing yours. Also, they are remarkably mobile and hard to catch. What with their sabbaticals, their archaeological digs, their work on exhibitions and lectures round the world and their periods of sick and maternity leave, it can take you a year to pin down the only man or woman whom you absolutely must consult about a particular piece of sculpture, or about the flower motifs on certain jewels or coins.

Even when these experts are present in the Museum, they cannot believe that a worm's time is of the slightest value. It is possible to make an appointment with an expert and to keep it to the minute to find that he has gone out, not just for the afternoon, but for a couple of days. Probably another, kinder man in the department will take pity on you and try to help, but the BM scholars are such specialists that he may be as much at a loss as you are. If his subject is, say, medieval French coins, he will not be able to locate the Greek coins, but will amiably pull out some trays at random and give you some books, and if you are clever you will winkle out what you want.

A surprising problem applying to my own book was that nobody in the Museum has or ever has had the slightest interest in plants. Whole guidebooks to the Museum have been written without the mention of so much as a daisy, let alone a cornflower, a common motif in jewellery, which the Museum consistently confuses with corncockle, a plant of a different family. I took a malicious pleasure in pointing out to several people that the plant was regularly misnamed on labels and in Museum books, but nobody bothered to make corrections. Nor could anyone identify the plants in the Assyrian reliefs. The learned answer was always, 'They are not real plants, of course, they are stylized', though there are ways of discovering what the plants depicted in the gardens of Nineveh and the rocky hills of Judah probably were. Luckily for me, I have a friend who is a botanist at Kew who consented to join me at the Museum for a morning where he smoothed out many a problem. Kew scholars are usually outgoing people – perhaps it is all that fresh air.

I am laughing a little at my experiences at the great seat of learning because humour alone sustained my spirits in frustrating moments. But looking back, I enjoyed the enterprise. I met with much kindness, much willingness to follow up a meeting with photocopies of obscure articles or pamphlets, many suggestions as to sources for reading. Some of the staff took such pride in their collections that they positively enjoyed showing them when they discovered that I was not a fool, and doubtless they get wearied with importunate visitors. If I could start again, I could write my piece much better than I did, for the research was spread over so long a period that I kept losing the thread while I turned to something else.

Still, it was a great adventure to come to me so late in my life, and I am grateful for it. When the work was done, I took Calypso to the Museum one morning, as you may remember, and had the pleasure of giving her the worm-feeling as I delivered a confident lecture on the Egyptian mummies.

Dead Letters

The most deeply felt writing of my life was the series of letters I wrote to Osbert after his death. You know me well enough to believe that there was nothing in the least spooky about this. I knew Osbert was dead and I had no ambition to 'get in touch with him' in a supernormal way. But his presence in our flat was still so strong that I would often look at his photograph and talk to it aloud and I would regularly sit down at my typewriter and write him a long letter. Since January of 1986, when Osbert had suffered a heart attack and conversation with him was increasingly difficult, I had kept an intermittent diary which was really conversations with myself, and after his death in July the diary turned into letters to Osbert. I would write every day at first, later perhaps twice a week, and after exactly a year I stopped altogether. I would slip each letter into a folder which I have not looked at since, not wishing to re-open old wounds, but I have not destroyed it.

Though I knew rationally that Osbert would never read them, these letters gave me intense consolation. I poured out all my feelings and unhappiness, but also gave him the day's gossip about our friends, telling him who had been specially kind to me (or unkind, but there were few of those, though some were tactless, harping on the unconvincing theme of a merciful release), and I reported the news of the day, including political incidents. I felt that Osbert would now, as always, want to be in the swim.

It is often said that nobody writes love letters any more, or other letters of emotion, either for lack of leisure or because the telephone is always handy, but I do not believe this. It may apply to the lost generation which, at school in the seventies and eighties, is almost illiterate, but I bet even they would write if they could. How many schoolboys have been spurred to write long, ill-spelt letters home because they were lonely? How many men away at a war have found words they did not know they knew to communicate with those they loved?

You may say that the telephone is the modern substitute for letters, and goodness knows the phone bills leap horrifically whenever somebody young is staying in the house. But I cannot believe that the quality of communication is the same, what with interruptions like, 'Aren't you ever going to finish?' from would-be phone users, and the nagging knowledge that every time you say, 'Darling, I long for you', you are chalking up another 50p. No, to the literate, letters are still best. If you are brought up in such a way that the written word is carved on your brain, enters your dreams, and occupies your mind whenever you are idle, you are not going to put it second as a means of communication to a piece of machinery intended solely for making arrangements. I have been in love three times in my life and each time my lover and I, when apart, would write and write and write, and I cannot believe that any buzz of the telephone can match the excitement of seeing a fat envelope in a well-loved writing plop through the letter-box on to the mat.

As I told you, I stopped writing those letters to Osbert a year after his death, but this was not a deliberate decision. I no longer needed to write, for the fading process of my sorrow had begun. For most people of normal sensibilities bereavement follows a close pattern, and to admit this implies no poverty of love. Many of the conventions of society observed by the bereaved are not foolish at all, but have evolved as consolations. For instance, for three months after Osbert's death I simply *could not* wear any bright clothes. One day I put on a red sweater, but promptly took it off again. The exaggerated funerals and mourning trappings of the Victorian age were a rather unpleasant self-indulgence, but at the centre of all the flummery of black horses and widow's weepers was a genuine need – that of the bereaved to withdraw a little from the world and have time for grief. 'To every thing there is a season.'

My reluctance to enter social life outlived my year's span of letter-writing. Although from the start I truly enjoyed dining with friends when it was, 'We won't ask anybody, it will be just us', it was perhaps two years before I could face a larger gathering.

My letters to Osbert were not my only writing during the year after his death. I wrote my book *Best Plants* for Conran-Octopus, which was timed to a tight schedule and needed a lot of research, but this was professional writing and I did not find it difficult. The writing which most seriously occupied my mind was of a different order, written not to commission, nor for publication, but for myself.

Dear Clare,

I warned you that it was an untidy life, perhaps because I am anything but single-minded. I wanted a career, love, children, friendship, travel, time to read, enjoy the arts, wander in the country and dig my garden, and if you pursue such heterogeneous pleasures you are unlikely to make millions or to be Prime Minister. I draw no moral from this. If I had concentrated my energies I might have reached higher goals, but I wouldn't have had such varied experiences or so much fun. I hope my story – now eighty years long – has interested you, the early part as a period piece, the post-war years as shedding a little light on your own life which, by the way, has unfailingly enriched my own.

Your loving Mother.

Index